MW00648591

Jack Hargreaves is amongst the best-known and most popular of television broadcasters. His weekly magazine programme about life in the country, 'Out of Town', was first broadcast in 1959 and ran for twenty-four years until 1981. Its appeal endures, and his country programmes continue to be nationally shown, most recently as 'Old Country'.

He was born in the West Riding of Yorkshire into farming stock, moving south as a boy to a farm in the Vale of Aylesbury. In 1929 he went to the Royal Veterinary College. By 1933 he was earning a living writing articles for Fleet Street and scripts for radio. He began working in films, first for Alexander Korda and later for Ealing Studios.

On the outbreak of War he joined the Royal Artillery, later being commissioned into the Royal Tank Corps and serving on Montgomery's staff. After the War, he returned to journalism, and in the early 1950s was editor of both *Lilliput* and *Picture Post*.

Always eager to reach as wide an audience as possible, he was inevitably drawn towards the television, then in its infancy. He joined Southern Television in 1959, both as a programme-maker on 'Out of Town' and as a Programme Controller. He now lives in Dorset.

In 1987 the Dovecote Press published the highly successful *Out of Town, a Life Relived on Television*, a first autobiographical volume about his childhood and early youth – which *The Old Country* succeeds.

THE OLD COUNTRY

JACK HARGREAVES

THE DOVECOTE PRESS

First published in 1988 by The Dovecote Press Ltd
Stanbridge, Wimborne, Dorset BH21 4JD

ISBN 0 946159 59 9

© Jack Hargreaves 1988

Printed and bound in Great Britain by
Biddles Ltd, Guildford and King's Lynn

All rights reserved

7   9   8

Contents

Introduction

In my grandfather's time Richard Jefferies wrote in one of his books about rural life that everybody in the cities had some connection with the countryside. Each had at least a grandmother who still fed the chickens. The industrial revolution had brought them comparatively recently to the towns.

Now it is the urban culture that is dominant, even though it may still be in the melting-pot. Seven-tenths of the people now live an urban life and they come down to the country seeking relief from it. Living in massed thousands, their food, shelter, warmth, sanitation, even their fun have to be organised for them. They can but pay and protest. In an idea of the Old Country they seek a glimpse of people doing things for themselves.

When I see a minibus of urban ramblers unloading alongside the road that runs over the hill – the road where Tess's horse was killed in Thomas Hardy's *Tess of the D'urbervilles* – I wonder about their names. They probably have ordinary English names – Mr Foster, perhaps, or Mr Hayward, Neate, Shepherd, Meade, Packer, Turner or Wainwright. All names that were earned by their ancestors in recognition of the jobs they did in the countryside.

If the old custom of naming people for what they do had lasted until now no doubt the people in the bus would be Checker and Driller and Coverage, Survey, Massage and Freeze. Together with Miss Currency Forklift who has married Sir Takeover Chip.

In my lifetime the long arm of progress had reached from the iron horseplough to the Exocet. The bulls have gone out of the retail trade and work on the production line of a big mail-order business. The downland turf – over which the hill road used to run – has been ploughed and injected with liquid nitrogen. The chickens almost never show their faces out-of-doors.

This book, like my other one *Out of Town*, is about living in the country more than fifty years ago. But this time it looks forward to consider the changes, and backward further into history to inspect the roots.

It may serve as background to some of the current notions about the preservation of the countryside.

Raven Cottage, Dorset
1988

1

Down by the River

During the scramble of 1940 we picked up a German Army pamphlet on leadership addressed to Non-Commissioned Officers. One maxim in it caught my eye – 'A soldier who is doing nothing is doing wrong'. It might just as well have been written by the Old Man. That was exactly his attitude. And that is why it was not he who introduced me to the lore of the river bank but my Quaker Uncle-in-Law. Uncle Stanley was an angler. The Old Man thought fishing was a particularly reprehensible way of doing nothing.

He rarely paid any attention to the river that flowed through the valley to which our own hills fell. He trotted over one of its bridges on the way to market; but only in the winter months would he give the scene his attention, at that time concerned to see how much water was lying on the flood-plain. He was interested in snipe.

Shooting snipe was one of his special abilities. It was a skill not given to many.

The long-nosed little snipe that feeds in the wet places springs up quite suddenly when disturbed and then flies away in a high-speed zig-zag which defeats almost all who try to shoot him.

Of course, the snipe developed this ability long before there were guns. It was his defence against the falcons. The falcon had learned that it was difficult to catch his prey in a straight race so he hovers at a height and, when he sees his victim on its flightline below, he goes into a power-dive. Coming down like a fighter aircraft he easily overtakes his prey and strikes it with his talons at the full velocity of his dive. But he has to set his course from above like a bomb-aimer and at the peak of his speed he doesn't have the steering to adjust to the zig-zag of the snipe.

I like to think of the falcon cursing in his frustration. I've heard some terrible language from men trying to shoot snipe.

The Old Man learned the art when he was a boy. Up on the moor when he went in search of hares and rabbits and the few wild grouse, there were many peat-hags – little patches of bog out of which one or two snipe would spring with startling suddenness. It was the old moor-keeper who taught him the trick and summarised it in a resounding phrase that I shall take the liberty of repeating.

Like so many wild creatures the snipe empties himself in preparation for flight, just before he zig-zags away. 'You hold on him till he shits', said the keeper, 'and when he shits you shoots.' For just that moment the bird flies in a straight line.

It makes it sound easy but there's more to it than the mechanics. You have to be of a character that is unflustered by the first sudden spring of the bird or the moment is over before you have recovered your composure.

So the Old Man was welcome down on the water-meadows when the snipe were in. He made the major contribution to the bag; and I suppose he was not above liking a chance to show off. In fact, he seldom shot in company. He didn't approve of shooting for sport and, although so expert, took his gun out only against creatures that were destroying his crops, or in search of a meal for the family.

So we quite often ate snipe and there is no question that they are delicious, but also a frightful lot of bother. You need about three to each person for a real meal and the plucking of them is long and fiddlesome. Mother expected everything to be brought to her kitchen-ready. The Old Man supported her in this but delegated the work in question to us. For me, the plucking of a dozen snipe for family dinner was only just made worthwhile by the delicious, strong juices that soaked down through the piece of toast on which each one of them was served.

Snipe are here today and gone tomorrow. They wander the width of the landscape looking for land that has been wetted just to their liking. Recently when, through a freak of the weather, our lawn was flooded, there were two snipe feeding on it at breakfast time for three days. Then they were gone. We never saw them before or since.

Up on the moor one or other of the peat-hags would usually be right for them, but these little patches only offered feeding room for a couple. Glancing over the bridge from his cart on Market Day, the Old Man was looking for wide stretches of land that had been flooded very shallow – somewhere around an inch of water – so that the snipe could work his long bill without getting his face wet. There used to be famous places like that over in Ireland – in Killarney, I think – where rich men kept shooting houses just so that for a week a year they could put on their waders and follow their setting-dogs over miles of the snipe bog.

Our greatest snipe memory of the Old Man concerns the last time of all that he shot them.

He was very old and too lame to walk more than a couple of yards on his two sticks. He hadn't been down to the river bank for years but on Market Day one of the low-ground farmers told us that miles of the flood-plain were in perfect condition and there were more snipe than the riverside men had ever seen before. So we made a plan.

We put him in a Windsor chair tied in a waggon and pulled him in stages across the upwind edge of the flood. Then, with the aid of many boys and a remarkable variety of dogs, we drove the floodlands towards him. It was some shoot! Of course, he couldn't tackle them the old keeper's way. They were travelling high and fast when they got over him, and beginning to swing right and left for the home places from which they had gathered. These driven snipe presented a different challenge altogether.

But he met it and in such a way that his memory lives still among the riverside families. He hardly said a word about it but he was smirking from ear to ear and, despite his customary temperance, allowed himself to be carried off to the pub to stand drinks all round.

Hardly anyone thinks of shooting snipe nowadays. For one thing, we don't have to develop such skills to get a variation of diet. Every kind of food from all over the world is in the town supermarket and many folks are well enough off to buy it by the trolley-load. Beyond that, the snipe are few because – as the conservationists will tell you – the amount of wetland is a fraction of what it used to be. And beyond that again, there are not a lot of people now who could hit them.

I told Mother all about the Old Man's triumph but, in truth, it made us both feel very sad. We remembered him when he strode tirelessly over the miles. I never went to the flood-plain with him again in winter, but in the summer-time I was often on the riverbank with Uncle Stanley and there I would listen to the snipe drumming.

This curious signal, coming at intervals like a monster bumble-bee, is the snipe's notification that you are in his territory at nesting time. He circles high overhead and seems to give a sort of sideways swoop as he produces the sound. This fact came up in evidence when 'drumming' became a matter of argument.

In Grandfather's time they took it for granted that the snipe produced the sound with his voice, but when I was young a group of naturalists alleged that it was caused by the tail. Two groups of short feathers on either side were stiffened outwards and, as he fanned his tail from side to side in a Japanese kind of way, they vibrated in the air to cause the effect. They said they had been able to demonstrate it experimentally.

I tried for myself. I took the short side feathers from the tail of a winter-shot snipe and stuck them in on either side of a cork, with a fishing-lead attached beyond. This rig, when whirled round the head in a six-foot circle, did produce a sufficiently recognisable echo of the drumming to convince me. particularly as, of course, the feathers in question would probablly be more developed in mating time.

There were many other birds on the river that didn't belong to our hills and moortops.

The coots – with their white bald patches visible from afar – had every yard of the water divided up into family properties. Once Stanley and I had fished a stretch for a bit I knew just where their territories were, even though the boundary marks were almost unnoticeable. I used to like to watch the cock coot from below come sneaking up to invade his neighbour's territory. The game seemed to be to get as far in as possible without being spotted, so he would choose a time when the owner was busy feeding. Suddenly there would be a splash and the proprietor would advance in a state of rage sounding his warning note, just like a cheap tin trumpet. The other fellow would scuttle away quite cheerfully as if to say, 'I had you there!'

The moorhens – 'water hens' in our district – who had

their white family-warning signals on their backsides instead of their foreheads, – seemed to have territories that
overlapped indiscriminately with the coots'. No doubt
there is a difference of diet, as with small birds that will
frequent different parts of the same tree.

They like to build their nests on a gravel-band offshore
or a tangle of boughs that had lodged in the river, anything
to get a stretch of water between them and dry land. They
want to protect their eggs from the rats, and quite right
because they are delicious. I have often hard-boiled two
or three in the billy-can in which we made the tea in order
to go with the fishing sandwiches.

Uncle Stanley taught me that the moorhen takes a great
risk with her nesting-site. In a high proportion of seasons
she gets things started nice and early, then the weather
breaks and the flooding river carries it all away. So I was
allowed to take eggs from an early clutch but once they'd
settled down to serious breeding they must be left alone.

I ran into this matter again much later when I was concerned with the question of gulls' eggs as human food.
They had always been regarded as a delicacy and were
gathered from the foreshore by local lads who put baskets
full on the train to the clubs and hotels in London. In the
atmosphere of nowadays this custom had come under severe
question.

On detached examination it proved that the Black-Head
gulls' first clutches are often laid on ground that will be
covered again by the highest Spring Tides, and at a time
when the spear-grass is not high enough to hide the nests
from the big Black-Backs.

It was decided to set a date each year up to which the eggs
could be taken, on the grounds that in fact the gulls main-
tained their numbers by means of the second broods. The

first year this happened we went out to inspect on a day that was hatching-time-plus-ten-days after the collecting stopped. Every nest had its quota of live chicks. There were no failures and no sign of a loss.

Uncle Stanley knew these things seventy years ago so I got a taste for moorhen's eggs. Again in the war, when I was leading a detached troop, there was in it a Berkshire gipsy called Harry Beasley who knew all about living in the fields. The sort of fellow of whom the Old Man would have said, 'God bless you, he'd eat where you'd starve'. I gave Harry a special place in the security system. I sent him out as a roving picket every morning at sunrise. We had plenty of rabbits and I used to have moorhen's eggs every morning at breakfast – all fresh and not yet 'youngked'. As a matter of fact they were the last I ever ate.

There is another bird whose nesting site is specially arranged in relation to the water, the dapper little Dipper. Like a big blackbird with a short tail and white waistcoat, he lives on water insects and, as these are active even before the frosts finish, they're available early. Not like most birds who have to wait until the land insects are active before they can feed young.

The dipper builds his early nest high enough to miss the floods but sticking out right over the water – on a root in the bank or a broken hatch or a hole in the wall of an old watermill. One year when I watched a nest every day I discovered why.

Most young birds leave the nest when they're ready to fly but the young dipper doesn't wait for that. He just tumbles out of the nest and finds himself in the water. There he swims naturally and hops over the stones to hunt the water insects. He learns to fly while at work, so to speak.

The dabchick builds right in the water, usually where the

willow twigs dip into the surface and can be used as an anchorage. She is a better shipwright than the water-hen and the nest floats very well. More than once I have known a nest to be torn free by the flood and carried off to lodge at another place downstream. Yet the process of hatching and rearing the brood went on undisturbed.

Like the puffin or the guillemot at sea, the dabchick spends most of his life under water, just popping up here and there for a breather. He'll dive as soon as he sees you and, if he knows you're about, he'll pop up somewhere under the cover of the sedges out of sight. If you are sitting still against a dark bush you can watch him unawares and then it's fun to try and point to the place where he'll pop up next. It's like a gambling game. More often than not, of course, he spots you before you're round the bend and disappears, leaving a flurry of bubbles and a circle rocking on the surface of the water. In this way he fools many trout-fishing beginners into thinking a big one has just risen.

But you have to be very quiet. In the country people often think they're watching for things when in fact the things are watching them. A lady said to the Old Man, 'How is it you and your lads are always seeing things?'

'If you sit down with your back to a tree trunk,' he told her, 'and don't make a sound or move a muscle for an hour, you'll see something you've never seen before.'

The heron is best of all at it. He stands up to his knees in the water quite unhidden, but he stands so still for so long that all suspicion is allayed. When a fish swims up close to his legs his bill goes down like a flash of light. All that time he keeps pin-point concentration. If only he had arms what a snooker player he would make! He reminds me of the great Fred Taylor who says 'You've got to fish all day as if you'd just missed a fish!'

I think the heron could keep that up all day. I've certainly watched him for an hour, peeping through the chinks in a bush I was fishing behind. At last I caught a fish and he was off with an angry 'cronk'. I think he was upset he hadn't known I was there.

Thus we learned to see things. The deeper we got into the countryside the quieter we were. Communicating with murmurs and gestures. Hissing to the dog, not whistling. No doubt it was on poaching that we polished the art.

When the town kids started to come down for outings you could hear them a mile away. The wild things disappeared at the distant sound of them. Consequently a lot of them thought the country was a dull place and usually tried to brighten it up with communal mischief.

Nowadays it's easy to tell the difference between town and country children. The country boy carries a stick. The town boy carries a clipboard. They come in large numbers accompanied by a teacher who – as seems necessary in all matters these days – carries a 'fact sheet'. One of our local landowners, keen to maximise his returns, did a deal for a schools outfit to develop a nature trail through his grounds. In order that the children should see something they put wild birds and creatures in coops along the way. Unfortunately the teacher neglected to feed them. The keeper got cross and turned them loose.

I think that the animal that most of all hates disturbance is the otter. The otter hates the human foot. Nowadays when the water-meadows are drained and the tractors work right up to the bank, and the places where we fished alone are constantly filled with competition anglers sitting fifteen yards apart, the otter is abandoning most of our larger rivers – making for the mountain streams and the quieter river estuaries.

Of course, they tried to blame it on the otter hounds. I never did like the otter-hunting myself but there's no doubt the otter would prefer being harried by it twice a year to a hiking population with leisure time to fill. Stopping the hunting has made no difference; the talk and activity devoted to otter preservation has not checked the exodus.

Stanley and I knew the otters well. We saw them often but we never knew when it would be, because – even without disturbance – the otter is a wandering creature. Only at breeding time do they seem to stay in one place. They fed along a stretch of water, leaving their 'spraints' – their droppings – at intervals along the bank. Then after a fortnight or so they vanished elsewhere. We knew they'd be back but we didn't know when.

But I have seen otters playing their famous game that has been described so often – choosing a clay bank of the right slope, shaking water onto it until it was a perfect slide, then climbing to the top and tobogganing down on their stomachs. Up and down, up and down, whistling with excitement.

Once when I had been fishing for several hours in a moored punt a young otter came swimming up alongside. I put down the landing-net and lifted him in. He spent five minutes sniffing all round the punt and managed to upset the bait-box, before slipping into the water again and swimming away.

Of course, they do take fish but most of all they like eels, which gobble up the spawn of the other fish species.

I once watched an otter in the pool below a mill-race turning over the big stones to catch the crayfish underneath, just as we used to do once a year for a crayfish dinner at the time of the Harvest Moon.

I think the things that will keep otters on a stretch of

river until they've just about exhausted them are the fresh-water mussels. They love them. At night they gather them up on the bank, always at particular feedings stations, and they are usually still feasting at dawn. They are very good at opening them, though this is not at all easy without a knife.

If they were disturbed and left a few unopened we received them with thanks. The freshwater mussel makes a very good bait for a big chub.

Uncle Stanley once found a small pearl in one of them – a very rare but not unknown happening. He had it made into a tiepin for Sundays and said that when he passed away he wanted me to have it.

If he ever recorded this wish my not-much-loved auntie managed to avoid mentioning it. Still, I suppose I must be thankful to her for bringing him into the family.

2

Out of Sight, Out of Mind

For every ten people who would know a robin on a Christmas card – or a blackbird, a blue tit, a bullfinch or a barn owl – there can be hardly one who would recognise five kinds of native fishes. And yet they are all around us in at least as great numbers as the birds.

Bird-watching is easy, watching wild animals is difficult and fish-watching even more so.

Still, it's a pity not to know about them. Uncle Stanley started to teach me about fish as soon as I was big enough to walk to the river.

'You've got to learn to think like a fish,' he said. Uncle Stanley was a thinking man. He was an electrical engineer and in those days the profession had some of the glamour that now attaches to the space scientist. He became one of the accomplished few who built the famous Battersea Power Station, now the subject of conservation. After that he took his skills around the world.

It takes an effort of imagination to feel like a fish. We fancy that with experience we can get into the minds of other warm-blooded mammalian creatures like ourselves. But the fish comes from an earlier world.

'The first thing to remember,' said Stanley, 'is that fish don't waste food on warming their blood, they keep it for energy and growth. So they feel the same as the water, and they behave according to the way the water's making them feel.'

He was the first man I ever saw use a water-thermometer

– long before it became a general angler's tool – and he
was interested in more than whether the current temperature was right for feeding. He checked always whether
the water was colder than the air, or the other way round,
to make up his mind if we were moving into a feeding
time or out of one.

Different kinds of fish vary in their feeding times and
details of this have been learned with the thermometer by
many anglers since Stanley's time. On a cold winter's
morning I once sat in a boat on the River Stour with Owen
Wentworth, Dorset's famous fishing postman. The water-
temperature was 40°F and Owen said, 'We might catch a
few chub. We won't get the dace until it makes forty-one
and we won't catch roach unless we make forty-two.' We
did catch chub and as the day wore on the thermometer
showed movement. We made the other two temperatures
as 12.30 and 2.15 – and in each case caught the fish in
question within ten minutes of achieving the reading.

Uncle Stanley showed me the anatomy of fish, including
a special technical component with which they are equipped
called the swim-bladder. This is a long, narrow gas-balloon
that runs parallel to the spine. The fish is able to draw
gases from the water to blow this up, or expel them in
order to deflate it. In this way he can tune his own
buoyancy so that he floats naturally at a particular depth
in the water.

Every good fisherman knows that the depth at which
his bait is set in the water is critical in each fishing situation.
Alterations of just an inch up and down can make a difference
to success. This is because the fish have found a supply
of food concentrated at one depth and have adjusted their
swim-bladder to keep themselves at that level.

'Look at that fish's face,' said Stanley, holding up a small roach on the first day he took me with him. 'Look at his face and tell me what's missing.'

'He's not got any ears,' I said.

'Ears! What good are ears under water! No, what else is missing? Look at his eyelids.'

'He's not got any eyelids, Uncle.'

'Quite right – no eyelids.'

Because a fish has no eyelids it is very shy of glaring light. Again, fishermen a half-century after Stanley's time have studied this fact in detail. Richard Walker started taking a light-meter to the water and demonstrated the light levels above which particular fishes will not feed.

In summer the best fishing for most fish is at dawn and dusk. I have often seen town angling clubs that have come down to fish a competition fail completely throughout a summer's day but begin to get fish at dusk when it's time for the coach to collect them. Even trout that rise to the surface flies in summertime return to the shade of the weeds when they are satisfied; and a carp lying high in the sunlit water will often be seen with his head tucked under a lily-pad.

The text of another of my Uncle's fishing sermons was 'Why do fish always face upstream?' Indeed they do face upstream. I had discovered already, while learning to watch fish, that if you move upstream you come from behind them and are less likely to be seen. The sermon supplied two answers. First, that it is easier for them to feed. Second, that it is easier for them to breathe.

Every item of fish-food in the water – water-fleas, shrimps, water-beetles, snails, mosquito larvae – lives its life trying to find shelter from the current, in the weedbeds and eddies and in the shelter of roots and stones. Every time it breaks cover for a moment it is washed an inch or two towards the sea. A fish that faces upstream, undulating his body just enough to hold himself in place, has this steady supply coming towards him. If he is a wise fish he will find a place where perhaps a channel between two banks of weed funnels this supply. The biggest fish are always to be found at the best fishing stations.

A fish breathes oxygen not from the air but from the water. It has no lungs. In fact, the first fish to develop lungs crawled out of the water to become the ancestor of all the rest of us.

Because he has no lungs a fish cannot draw a breath as we can and then expel it. He takes out the oxygen through a branching arrangement of gill-rays set on either side of his throat. These are covered by hinged trap-doors called the gills.

So now the fish must find some way of breathing – some way of creating a continuous current of water through the gills.

In still water he does this by moving around. He wanders endlessly, opening mouth and gills alternately to pass water through. People know this without knowing that they know it. Ask a friend to imitate a goldfish. He will open and shut his mouth in a regular rhythm.

In the river a fish first faces upstream. Every time he opens his mouth the current of fresh water flows in.

'Now notice,' said Uncle Stanley 'if we show ourselves to those fish lying there they will bunk downstream.' Whoops – downstream they go as fast as they can; and as soon as they're safely away they whip round and face upstream again. He goes very fast, not only to escape danger but also because he can't breathe en route. He's running away from the current of water; and if he tried to open his mouth to force some through it would act all too effectively as a brake.

So a river fish hates facing downstream. A big fish on the hook can be brought to surrender twice as fast if you can hold his head in that direction. 'He's drowning, you see,' said Uncle Stanley. How many people know you can drown a fish?

It was at this stage in his instruction that Uncle Stanley called for a performance of our well-known duet rendition of 'Ilkla Moor baht at' in thirds. Choosing a place on the bank where fish were to be seen we sang our hearts out. It had no apparent effect on them at all. 'You see,' he said, 'they can't hear you. Yet you see townies down here fishing who whisper to one another, as if they were on a rabbiting trip.' Then he would stand up and gently bump his heel on the bank. The fish were gone downstream. If you drop a matchbox on the bottom of a boat, he would explain, you will scare off every fish for twenty yards.

Sound-waves pass reluctantly through water, so a fish is equipped to perceive even the tinest waves of changing water pressure caused by things moving in the stream. Along each side of the body runs a nerve which is connected at frequent intervals to nerve endings in the skin. With these he can feel small movements in the water at a long distance. On account of these, the food-fish knows that he must remain motionless in the weeds or the predatory fish will feel his presence. The nerve endings are far enough apart to give him an accurate bearing. It is probable that – in a 'sonar' way – he can feel his own movement reflected from obstacles and so find his way in the dark.

This beautiful apparatus is known as the 'lateral line'. You can trace its row of dots along the flank of a fish. Uncle Stanley called it the fishes' live sides. And so did D. H. Lawrence; he used the phrase in a poem he wrote about a pike.

My uncle also thought that fish are concerned with the general pressure of the water. This, he said, was the truth of the old angling rhyme.

When the wind is in the West,
  Then the fishes bite the best.
When the wind is in the South
  It blows the bait in the fishes' mouth.
When the wind is in the East,
  Then the fishes bit the least.
When the wind is in the North
Then the angler goes not forth.

Stanley was scornful of it. How does a fish know which way the wind is blowing? It's just that for us, living in the air, the winds are associated with the different pressure systems of the weather. Down where the fish are it's the pressure that matters, whether the wind blows or not.

Within a few days of telling me this he found a shoal of big roach. For two days they were on the feed almost continuously. On the third day we couldn't catch them but, lifting our baits a foot, we caught chub. There was hardly any wind all through but, on the second night, the barometer showed a noticeable rise.

The roach, which feed strictly on the bottom, had to rise in the water a bit to find a comfortable pressure, and thus went off the feed. The chub, which feed at all levels, still found food without discomfort. As people say nowadays – it's arguable.

All these, and a hundred other things, my uncle taught me about the physical nature of fish – but also something about the sociology of fish. How the predatory fishes had their territories. How the trout in a river will share out the feeding-stations strictly according to rank; so that if you catch the biggest fish, the next in size will quickly move into his place, having always had his eye on a move to a better position. How the shoal fish – roach and dace and chub – do everything together and share common emotions, coming on the feed together or going onto a state of fright together: but how – even within such sheep-like communities – you will catch the little fish first. The wiser and larger ones will watch the food sampled by their juniors before accepting it themselves.

We watched this happen one day in a swim of clear water where we had put our groundbait, and where the arrangement of the willow-trees controlled the light just right for us to see the gravel bottom.

The shoal had arranged itself downstream in order of size, with the little ones first nosing up to the groundbait. Then came the next size, and the next. As each size moved in, the lesser ones gave way. By carefully reserving our hook-baits we achieved our ambition of catching the biggest roach first.

In the light of all these considerations Uncle Stanley planned my fishing lessons. In the winter we wouldn't go out till middle-day when the water had warmed a little. In the summer we fished in the cool of the morning and evening, with a long lie in the grass in between when we ate our pasty and parkin and drank cold tea from a bottle. Then Stanley lit his pipe and settled down to some more of his thinking and I went looking for birds-nests.

The collection of eggs that I made as a child would now be illegal but then birds-nesting was a recognised habit for country boys. Even so, my uncle was very strict about egg-taking.

He wouldn't allow an egg to be taken from a nest with less than four in it. 'Birds can only count up to three,' he said.

'How did you get to know that, Uncle?'

'By experiment and observation, lad. I never saw a bird desert a nest with three eggs in it. If you leave them but two they'll abandon them. Anyway we were like that our-selves long ago. The black fellows in Ozzie can only count One-Two-Three-Many.'

I expect that now, seventy years later, the Aborigine children in Australia go to school with calculators.

Also in the dog-hours of the summer days I would catch grasshoppers. It is difficult to imagine now how they swarmed in the riverside grass, with the air filled with the noise of them scraping away on their thousands of tuneless fiddles. I got to be very good at catching them in my cap. With them it was possible, even in the hottest hours, to catch the lazy high-lying chub. We did it by the tedious, old-fashioned method of 'dapping', exactly as described in *The Compleat Angler*. This was the only time that we fished according to the instructions of Isaak Walton. Other-wise we regarded him as out-of-date and ill-informed. There is some justification for our low opinion of that sage which I will leave for later.

Also to keep me busy in the afternoons my uncle would cut me a long willow-twig and split it down an inch at the small end to make a springy fork. This was the implement he specified for the capture of 'tunnel-bugs' – the larvae of caddis flies. These swarmed in the ditches that drained down from the riverside fields. Naked, they look like cater-pillars but they have sticky sides to which they can attach camouflage. Thus some of them cover themselves with grains of sand; some make their tunnels of tiny gravel; others chose tiny twigs and morsels of dead leaf. Only the head emerges at the front, together with a group of strong front legs with which they drag themselves along.

There is a knack in squeezing them from the tail and

pushing out the worm. In those days it was a favourite bait for roach and I could sometimes sell our surplus to other fishermen at four for a penny.

Not nowadays. Nowadays all the old tricks and tips for fishing baits are out-of-date. The millions of urban anglers can go to shop for a half-gallon of factory-bred maggots and a plastic bag of ready-mixed ground bait.

We sometimes had maggots, but had to obtain them by a method that was not wholly approved at home. After we got indoor sanitation I would hang a dead rabbit in the old privy. The bluebottles struck it and the maggots grew and then dropped into a bucket of sand beneath. So what? For generations people had been walking on the upwind side of that place.

Sometimes we would hang a dead rabbit right over the river, where it could be well-hidden in a willow bush. The news would get round and it would become a gathering place for fishes all interested in the chance of a maggot – which we would then supply with hook in it.

This situation arose naturally with the elderberries. Roach are very fond of them. They would gather under an elder-bush that overhung the water, when the berries were ripe and the wind was blowing. Every year we got one or two chances for elderberry fishing.

Carp like boiled new potatoes. A ripe cherry will catch a chub. But usually when chub fishing was in mind I would go to the slaughter-house on Market Day to collect a tin of greaves. This is a white stringy substance from the inside of the beasts that I used to boil white and cut up small. Stanley was never quite satisfied. He said the best greaves used to come from the tallow-maker; but by the time I was around the candles were made of paraffin wax.

All in all, the most frequent and overall the most productive bait was bread-paste. It had to be made with real home-baked bread – and even then there was a secret knack to it.

You took a half-loaf to the waterside; then you pulled out as much of the inside as you could hold in your hand, dipped it in the water and then squeezed it dry before kneading it. The trick was that all the water and all the air had to be pressed from it in a single squeeze. If you released and squeezed again, it would suck in air like a sponge and it would never have the proper texture.

Stanley, of course, could make better paste than I could. But Bobby Cooper was the man. He had only one arm, which over the years had developed the strength of two. So when Bobby came fishing with us, out of his great right hand came the best bread-paste of all.

We used to catch a lot of fish in those days. But why did we go to so much trouble to catch all those fish that we wouldn't eat? One summer's afternoon, after a spell of thought, Uncle Stanley delivered his opinion. 'Life is best,' he said, 'when spent in the pursuit of understanding and the exercise of skills.'

So that, I thought, is how he manages to get along with Auntie.

3
The Walnut Tree

'Before long' said my Television Friend, 'you will be able to watch twenty-four channels.'

'But it's crazy to devote all those resources to twenty-four television channels!'

'Ah well', he said, 'you can't stop progress.'

It is difficult to decide when it first occurred to man that he could master the whole physical world. I think it must have been quite recently because the idea never reached Grandfather. He didn't set out to conquer Nature but felt himself to be in a mutually respectful partnership. If he sent us out to put up a line of barbed wire to keep cattle out of the hedge he would never have a nail driven into a tree. If an oak tree stood in the way of the line we had to put two extra posts out of line to get round it. No nails in trees.

He wanted everything that he did to the landscape to be done perfectly. After a field was ploughed he would send us out with a garden spade to dig the corners where the plough couldn't get. In the Old Man's view Grandfather wasted a lot of time fiddling with things that didn't contribute to profit. After all, where the plough couldn't go the drill and the binder couldn't either, and such little corn as grew in the corners went to the pigeons and the flocks of finches. That was alright with Grandfather.

Once a wild foxglove seeded itself in the bank below one of the hedges. It was a place from which water would naturally drain away, and the season it grew there turned into a drought. Every day for a fortnight he carried a bucket of water over from the yard and gave it a soaking. Grandfather loved foxgloves whose proper home was in the woods. The Old Man's heart was in the grazings but Grandfather was really a man of the woods. Even in our small woodlands there were so many things that needed to be done right.

The most obviously orderly thing that happened in the woods was the copsing – that's how we said it, though 'coppicing' was the way it often got spelled.

A copse is a plantation in which particular species are harvested not as full-grown timber but at the sapling stage, anything from three to eight or ten years old. The copse wood served a hundred uses in country life and the maximum crop of it was achieved by 'stooling' the roots. Planted just a few yards apart and when they had grown their first sapling stems, cut down to the ground. From the root came a bunch of several stems and as these grew and were cut in successive years, the root of the stool became lumpy and mature, until each stool would yield fifty and more stems.

The copsing species were the hazel above all and secondly the ash; chestnut sometimes and where the wood was damp, a few stools of alder. Some birches were stooled for the broom-makers. There were willow copses down by the river and these were cut annually by the basket-makers, so that they grew rods by the score and in winter when the bark was red would look like a crowd of punk hair-dos.

With us, the stools were not in separate copses as they are in some districts, but formed the underwood of the old-fashioned mixed woodland. By that I do not mean a mixture of broadleaved trees and conifers. The top timber trees were oak and beech, with a few sycamores and

Spanish chestnut that were grown big to be planked by Great Uncle Harry. He was a master woodworker and his tradition in the family was as strong as the farming one. On small farms where only one son can take over there was usually another craft to be inherited. On Mother's side they were farmers and weavers. My Uncle Alfred Jubb had risen to be a Tackler, which is what the top master-weaver was then called.

When Great Uncle Harry was first a journeyman he put his tools on the back of a black pony and walked off in the company of a little running-dog called Fly. Like Jude the Obscure he was a true journeyman. At last he found himself needed in Lincoln where he worked for a long time on the altar-screen in the Cathedral.

In honour of Harry and his predecessors we grew at each of the corners of our woodland – planted there perhaps because they needed light – a group of box trees. Most people know Box only as the material for little clipped hedges or topiary bushes, but these were of a small timber size, large enough for one of the lower branches to be turned by Harry into a polished wooden spill-jar. Many times I have filled it for Grandfather, folding the long spills that he poked in the fire to light his pipe from the pages of *Farm, Field and Fireside*. The home-grown boxwood was used for the block-planes that my great Uncle made for himself, for rulers, squares and the handles of the chisels that he endlessly sharpened. Harry used to say that for every ten men that could use a tool only one could put a perfect edge on it.

All his beautiful tools were kept in a chest he had built himself which – having no family of his own – he said was coming to me.

However, my Uncle Willie – who was a somewhat over-dapper chap who waxed his moustaches – sneaked it away when he emigrated to America – I never saw him again. Unlike my Uncle Holmes who had gone to Canada. As soon as war broke out he came back to join up. He died just after dawn on the first day of the Battle of the Somme – his first day in action.

Uncle Willie didn't come back. He was in Fall River City, Massachussets, sitting on my box. Mother said I ought to forgive him, and I suspect she had colluded in order to help him on his way in the New World. But, although he took our other tradition to America, I always hoped he did not encounter too much prosperity.

The tall trees in the woods re-seeded themselves, dropping their acorns and mast and spinning winged seeds. Grandfather kept his eye on where they had germinated. They were allowed to grow big enough for decent fencing posts and then the unwanted pulled out with the plough-chains and a team of four. When I began to get muscles, at about the age of twelve, it was my job to stand with an axe to cut the roots that wouldn't come away.

Those that grew close to larger trees that would soon come to felling would be allowed to grow on, and because they wanted to reach the light that filtered to them through the canopy above they, like the copse-wood below, would grow tall and straight.

The big trees were felled when they were in their prime, before they showed any signs of old age.

Nowadays, if such a tree were to be felled the forester would be roundly abused by those who believe they exist simply for the pleasure of the uncultivated eye. But these native hardwoods were then the raw material of industry, on their way to the coach-builders and bridge-builders and the makers of gun-carriages, river barges, locks and barns and hatches. Grandfather knew that alongside each one already stood its successor, each one the descendant of trees cultivated the same way in the same place since the days of the Lords of the Manor.

They were felled with the axe and the cross-cut saw. The bigger limbs went to the waggonwrights and boat-builders. The lesser limbs were the main raw material for the charcoal-burners. Then as the big trunks lay there the barkers came to the woods, mainly women. The axe-men would cut a slit all along the top side and into this they thrust their small, square barking irons. The bark was levered off in big sheets and loaded to go to the tannery.

Thus the trunk was naked when it was winched up onto the timber bob and hauled away by the timber-man's team – anything from eight to twelve heavy horses. Grandfather would allow this to be done only when the ground was frozen hard. He fussed and bothered to make sure that as little damage as possible was done. The timberman was very patient with him. In any case his team was so responsive to each word he spoke that the whole thing was done as neatly as one man pulling a handcart.

Now and again it would happen that two or three big trees were felled at a time when the copse below had also been cleared. For a season or so there would be a patch of full sunlight on the woodland floor. The result was something to remember.

I remember when I was very little Grandfather lifted me into the float. 'We'll drive us up to Long Wood where 'twas cut', he said. 'That'll be like a garden.' It was a garden; the whole sunlit patch was a mass of flowers – green, pink, white and yellow. The sun had warmed the roots and bulbs and resting seeds to produce a sight that I've only seen three of four times since.

The copse work was all done in the winter-time. The various woodmen would walk the woods in the fall with Grandfather and make a bargain for the stools they were to clear.

There was an old clog-maker from one of the mill-towns who came to us only now and again when we had an alder stool grown really big. All the soles of the mill-girls' clogs were cut from alder, nearly two inches thick, very light and not easily rotted by the damp puddles. After the leather upper had been nailed on with a close row of dome-headed tacks each sole was shod with iron, like a pony's foot.

The man who made chestnut pale fencing wanted two to three inch stuff. He cut all his rod into pieces of fence height and then divided each one of them into three with a beautiful little triple-wedge splitter made from yew-wood.

Every year the broom-maker came to us and all other places where he could get what he wanted – young, feathery birch. He would be pleased if he got his pony-float full of tightly-tied bundles, and then went on to his other sources until by Spring there was a pile of them as big as a haystack in his broom-yard. All summer he sat with his family making besom brooms. A lad barking the hazel handles. A little girl splitting ribbons of hazel to bind on the birch. They must have belonged to some sort of a guild, the broom-makers, because when in autumn they went off to sell their year's production they each went to a different town and none would poach on the other's territory. Our lot went to Derby. It seemed an enormous journey but, when their waggon was loaded up as high as a house with brooms, they went off in great spirits and slept under the waggon on the way in order not to waste money. They came back cheerful too, the year I remember them returning.

The waggon was empty and they had averaged fourpence a broom! Now they all had new caps on, the leaf had fallen and it was back to the woods for some more feathery birch.

These specialist craftsmen used to come and do their own wood work, but every year Grandfather's biggest deal was with the man who cut the hazels. This was the biggest copse crop and he was a man who produced a dozen different products for different people to use.

His name was Mr Bowman and that is still a common name in many parts of Britain for families who have had the trade of woodman. No doubt this is because they once also produced the staves for the long-bows. There were still a few yew-trees here and there in our woods to give evidence of it. Now they were ancient but, even when they were young, I don't see how you could stool them to produce rods. Perhaps the bow-staves were split from bigger planks?

The Bowman family were expert in all the things that could be done with hazel and something of their work went into every home every year. They made the neat bundles of peasticks, laying the untrimmed rods neatly in the three forks of a 'horse' made from driven stakes, and throwing over the piece of old plough-chain that hooked onto a pedal and held everything tight while the bundles were tied; they trimmed long rods for bean-poles and for splitting by the oldest son who made the plaited wattle bundles. All the waste – a big proportion of the whole – was made into tight faggots. A load of these was always a part of their bargain with Grandfather as fuel for our copper.

The whole Bowman family worked together. They seemed to develop their real identity in the woods. At home – where once or twice I had to take messages to them – they seemed not so much at home, but when winter took them to the woods each seemed to have his inherited place in the copsing order.

In a shelter on the southern edge of where they were clearing – built from the first faggots of the season – sat the oldest of them. In front of him grew a pile of thatching spars, each one split, pointed at both ends and then given a lengthwise twist of just the right power. The thatcher could then bend them over double and push the points in close together – like a hair-pin.

One year he was under pressure producing spars. A rich American had decided to have his mansion thatched in the English manner. The master-thatcher who had been tempted over to do it had placed an enormous order and spars grew up around the grandfather Bowman. He shouted at anyone who came near – 'Theesun spars be going off on a steamer!'

He worked with a little, light billhook with a razor-sharp edge. He called it his 'sparrook'. A long line before him had inherited it each in turn when they handed over the work that needed stamina and muscle. He made a collection of ash rods of just the right length and thickness and stood them in a barrel of water alongside the shelter. When soaked each would be dressed and worked into a perfect circle which would then dry hard into shape. Several sacks of these went to the coast each year to be sewn to the fishing boat sails as mast rings. He made the pyramid traps that the keepers needed for catching pheasants, and gave a couple to Mother for snaring the barnyard cockerels that were needed for dinner. He could also make a remarkably efficient pair of nutcrackers from a single hazel rod.

Gradually over the clearing worked the Bowmans who were in their prime. Each stood, legs wide apart, swinging a heavy hook made by the blacksmith under his own super-vision; and each swearing that he could never work with the clumsy thing used by the man next to him.

Mother Bowman cleared up and gathered the faggot stuff, assisted by a number of toddling Bowmans whose job was also to feed sticks into the fire over which, on a tripod of rods, hung their iron pot. You could always tell where woodmen were by looking for the wisp of smoke that rose through the trees from their clearing.

They all knew the woods as well as the badgers and squirrels did, every movement and every sound. Even the littlest Bowman, who still lay in a basket hung in the shelter alongside the sparrook man, knew the calls of the wood-land birds. The Huntsmen consulted them on the move-ment of foxes. The keeper valued their help in finding all the pheasants' nests when hatching time came around. Grandfather often went up there to take a mug of tea in the shelter. He called it 'The Sparrook Arms'.

He liked to look over the clearing and see that, as always, it had been done right. The cut stools lay like spiky pincush-ions. Every rood had been cut at the same height and at the same sharp angle that would shed the rain. Every branch and twig cleared away and sent to its proper use.

I'm sure he thought it was all going on for ever. His great-grandfather had known the Bowman great-grandfather. He was sure that we his grandsons would give the woods our care and maintain the intricate rotations, and that we would have a Bowman grandson to pour us a mug of tea.

But then the first blow came; and, extraordinarily, it was struck by the Portuguese.

When war came the Portuguese were the only little nation with the courage to declare on the Allied side. To express their support they even sent one battalion to the Front.

We heard about it from Uncle Alfred Jubb when he came on leave. He said it caused a sensation. The news of their arrival went the whole length of the Allied lines in a day because – to the astonishment of Tommy and Poilu – they had brought their women with them!

They turned up in our district a year later, but I don't remember them bringing any women. Perhaps they thought that, with nearly all our lads away, they would be alright. In that first Great War the men of the countryside went off. I know one little village now with a war memorial that records the death of all the young men of the place on a single day.

With submarines all around us and the factories roaring away to supply the biggest armies ever known, the country needed hard woods as never before. So they brought over the Portuguese woodmen.

Trees and trees and trees were felled. Nobody cared whether a tree had come to its turn, or whether another stood ready to take its place.

I sat on a bank in little short trousers and watched a great Portuguese team of eight horses hammering up the flint roads over Lines' Hill. The crash of the horse shoes and the groans of the big timber-bobs loaded with a giant beech trunk, with the strange shouts of men heard, for the first time in my life, in a foreign language.

I didn't think they would make it: but they did. They knew their job. And they did some job. There has never been any real supply of seasoned native hardwoods in Britain since. Grandfather watched and knew that the old system could never be restored. Nothing could be done right again. He had always been a quiet man and now he became a sad one. Instead of nurturing continuity he began to meditate on the coming changes. The war had been a great stimulation of progress.

Perhaps that's why he drank. There were some who said that he drank himself to death. Still, he did last until he was ninety-one.

The last thing he ever planted was a walnut tree. Every farm had a walnut tree, usually two or three growing on in rotation. A walnut takes a long time to grow. Each one in turn provided the crop and then, grown to its maximum, it was worth a lot of money from the gunsmiths and the furniture makers.

Grandfather said a man must plant a walnut tree for his grandchildren, not for a tax benefit in his own lifetime. So he planted his last one.

We used to knock down the nuts with a very long pole, as the Spanish do their olives. In doing it we broke many of the tip twigs and they grew again in larger numbers. 'A woman and a spaniel and a walnut tree: the more you beat them the better they be'. Find me a farm now where kids can knock down walnuts for their mothers to pickle.

You can find a bit of copsing here and there but most of the stools are overgrown and in decay. I think that may be why we have seen such an increase in roe deer. They love the copse wood but earlier the Bowmans and their like gave them no peace in wintertime. And it may be the reason why the dormice, which the woodmen used to give us as pets in the days before hamsters and gerbils, are in contrast disappearing. The dormice like things as they used to be.

There are here and there patches of the old mixed woodland in some sort of order. But ninety acres close to me have just been bulldozed out and replaced with young conifers, with a large subsidy per acre and a tax benefit to come. Who cares that they will produce softwoods at a price dearer than we can buy them off the Baltic ships coming into Kingston-on-Hull.

Grandfather wouldn't have liked lifeless firwoods covering our hillsides. 'And he wouldn't have wanted to watch twenty-four channels of television.

4
The Art of Pure Deceit

For several million years the world prepared itself to provide the perfect pleasure that I enjoy each season from May until September. It is an experience that can be had only in those months of the year, and in very few places.

As the planet began to cool it also began to shrink and became too small for its outer covering which, in consequence, wrinkled like the skin of a rotting apple. In this way some of the once-molten rocks were buckled up to make ranges of hard mountains.

Many times this happened, producing many different rock formations. During the intervening climate changes the sea – deep and shallow in turn – covered the earth in different patterns and the deposits from the bed of it were buckled up as sand stones and shales.

In some of these oceans tiny creatures bred in unimaginable quantities and deposited on the bottom their minute shells and skeletons. It was this white mass that rose up in the last mountain-building period, and there appeared on earth for the first time the softly rounded shapes of the chalk hills.

It was all Nature's great plan to give pleasure to me and some of my friends.

The rain that falls on the Chalk Hills – on Salisbury Plain, the Hampshire and Dorset Downs, the South Downs and the Chilterns – behaves in a special way. It does not, like mountain rain, rush down over the rocks to the sea in unfishable torrents. Nor, like the rain on clay lands, does it run down the surface field-drains to fill a whole valley with a flood as muddy as lentil soup.

The rain on the downlands sinks through the grass into the chalk and then, for a whole season, it settles downwards until – meeting an impermeable layer lower down – it breaks out of the lower edge of the downs in sparkling springs.

Three things happen to the water on its way down. First, it is filtered free by the chalk of all impurities. Second – its chemistry becomes mildly alkaline and so is perfect for supporting life. And thirdly it takes on the subterranean temperature of between 48 and 50 fahrenheit. So the resulting chalk streams are clean, rich, cool in summer and never freezing in winter time.

Then, long before there were men on earth came the entrance of the leading character in this production: the trout.

The trout was a fish that originally lived in the sea, but once a year entered the estuaries and rivers to lay the spawn from which its young hatched and lived in safety until strong enough to return to the ocean. Working gradually further upstream on their annual trips for this purpose the trout reached the chalk streams where they emptied into the coarser rivers below. There they discovered food enough summer and winter to make the return to the sea unnecessary. In a perfect world of crowfoot and ranunculus, and minnows, water-shrimps and crayfish, of a marvellous miscellany of waterflies whose larvae are hatched in the alkaline water, they decided to stay. So developed the wild, freshwater Brown Trout. In the minds of the cognisant it is reckoned the most distinguished fish in the world.

Sometime in the seventeenth century came an invention

which was Man's first contribution to the perfection of these arrangements – the development of water-meadows. On the lower stretches of the chalk streams the riverside land was levelled and the height of each stretch of the river was made controllable by the building of hatches.

The land was turned into a patchwork of little meadows divided by drains which all led to larger 'draughts' through which the water could be returned to the river lower down.

Early in the year when the chalk springs ran fullest, the intricate pattern of hatches was manipulated to flood each patch of meadows in turn. The chalk water would lie there warming the frost out of the ground and dropping the alkaline silt. When it was drained off the water-meadows sprouted with a wonderful 'early bite' of grass that brought food for sheep and bullocks weeks earlier than on the rest of the land. In the later Spring and up to June further floodings brought the finest crops of hay.

The whole of this intricate system – reminding one, perhaps, of films of the irrigation channels in the Nile Valley – was handled by special craftsmen known as the 'Drowners', or in some places the Meaders or Meadmen. Because the hay mowing machines could not be taken in over the main drains, they preserved the high art of mowing with the scythe. They were proud men – like most country craftsmen – and proudest of all, perhaps, in the Kennet valley since from there the Drowners were fetched three times a year in Royal waggonettes to mow the old Queen's grass at Windsor Castle.

At the times when the ditches were at their fullest and the Drowners carried long poles on their shoulders it was an odd sight to watch them making their way in a long series of pole-vaults over each deep drain in turn.

Down among the water-meadows the trout were biggest.

The ditches gave shelter to young fish. The hatches produced big splash-pools in which the larger ones grew. And the passage of the water on and off the land produced the richest feed.

It was here that in Queen Victoria's reign there developed a form of fishing that may be called 'The Cult of the Dry Fly'.

The ephemeral flies that hatch in the river – the Olive, Iron Blue, Pale Watery, the Mayfly and others – are greatly loved by trout. As the 'nymphs' or grubs of various kinds rise to the surface, each in its season, they transform themselves into flies and take to life in the air. From the time they leave the shelter of the weeds until they fly away the trout feed on them.

The Dry Fly fisherman watches for when the fly breaks the surface and the trout rises to snatch it back again. He seeks to place an artificial fly lightly on the surface – an artificial fly with a hook in it. To perform the act perfectly it is necessary that the angler should know on just which fly the fish is feeding and present him with an accurate impersonation of it. So say the purists.

To carry out this immaculate deception great skills are needed.

First the casting of the fly so that it drops as light as thistledown just ahead of the nose of a trout lying fifteen yards away. Obviously you cannot cast an artificial fly. The thing weighs no more than a postage-stamp and if you tried to throw it it would stop within a yard of your hand and then flutter to the ground. So you must cast a heavy line that can be manipulated like a whiplash. Gradually special rods were designed for this task – first of heavy greenheart wood, then of split and laminated cane, of fibre-glass, carbon fibre and finally boron. Some of these rods became famous in the names of the gentlemen who specified them.

Then the lines, which were spun in turn from horsehair, silk and then man-made fibres, were perfected in suppleness, colour and floatability. Their heavy parts were placed at different points along their length in order to perfect the rolling action that would carry the fly forward. At the front a tapered transparent 'cast' – originally of silkworm gut – kept the sight of the line from the fish.

And then the famous artificial dry-flies. These, it was insisted, must be floating portraits of the real, live flies. They were made by tying pieces of bird feather and animal fur to tiny hooks – game cock, starling, French partridge – badger, squirrel and the hair from a hare's ear – these and many more. To these were devoted experiment, much theorising, and endless splenetic argument. In this 'exact imitation' period the sport got quite nasty!

The arrogant Dr Halford produced his own series of fly-dressings, laid down the law and managed to dominate most of the fraternity. But some wouldn't have him. Exasperated with Halford, Sir Herbert Maxwell ordered all his flies tied bright scarlet all over, and showed that he could catch as many trout as any. The shy, studious Skues experimented with catching the fish in the larval stage, just as they rise to the surface to hatch into flies. This 'nymph' fishing infuriated Halford so much that, despite lifelong friendship, he refused ever to speak to Skues again.

Poor Halford, his perfect imitations didn't catch many fish. He had mistakenly assumed that the mind and the eyesight of the trout were just like his own.

Most important of all, aside from these technical matters, is knowledge of the trout and its environment, and of those other creatures who share it. It was to this that minds were chiefly devoted during the serene and happy period that

THE ART OF PURE DECEIT

followed when the quarrel between Halford and Skues was forgotten. This was the golden age of the Dry Fly and the time when I first met it.

We had no such waters in the North and no such techniques, but soon after coming south to College I was driven by a friend to the water-meadows of the Kennet valley. You can guess the date near enough because he had just taken delivery of a new Bull-nosed Morris.

It was the third of June and I had never seen a Mayfly. As we pulled over the canal bridge beside the river the world was full of Mayflies. Bull-nosed Morrises did not have windscreens in those days but if there had been one we could have used it to see our way through the great cloud of glinting gossamer fragments that danced up and down in the still air up-wind of every bush and tree. I never saw anything like it; nor did I again because I think it was just another part of Nature's grand design to drop me there at the time of the greatest Mayfly hatch in living memory.

By the end of the afternoon I knew the life-history of the Mayfly and had seen it in all its stages.

The May Dance that was happening in the sun that day was first made up of a mob of fluttering females, all ready for what can happen as a result of going to dances. The males first approach from beneath. On this depends the whole character of the performance because the males have eyes on the top of their heads. Thus they fly upwards through the cloud, examining all they pass, and then drop to the bottom again to start another rising inspection. The hovering of the females and the leaping of the males combine to great effect.

Dancing is followed by mating. After mating the male hands his cards in and drops to float dead and spread-eagled on the water. Then he is known as a 'spent', and trout will sometimes, but not often, develop a taste for 'spents'. The Colonel used to tie a good copy of them with badger-hair.

The female meanwhile flies upstream dipping her tail in the water every yard or so to release a little clutch of eggs. Little trout will leap to try and catch her as she does so. Big trout know better. When, a quarter of a mile or so higher up, she completes her laying then she, too, falls to join the 'spents'.

The creature that hatches from the egg on the river-bed is called the nymph. For a year it grows, feeding on minute vegetable rubbish, and keeps changing its skin like a lobster to gain space to grow bigger. The next year, usually on a day in June, it rises to the surface, splits down the back and emerges as a fly which rides for a moment on the skin of its former self to stretch its wings. That is usually the moment in the year when fly, fish and fisherman meet.

But there's more. That first-day fly is soft and dull-green and rather clumsy. We call it the 'Green Drake'. It settles for the night on waterside vegetation and when the sun shines tomorrow it will perform a miracle. It splits down the back again and out of one fly climbs an entirely new one, wings, legs and all. This time it is bright silver-grey, crisp, smooth-winged and very agile. We call it the 'Grey Drake' – or the 'Spinner' because by tea-time it will be dancing and by evening it will be dead.

It is one of the wonders of Nature that when that female Spinner lays her eggs she will fly upstream. The eggs will be carried downstream as they sink. For a year the nymph will be washed downstream every time he loses his grip on the bottom. When he rises to the surface to hatch, downstream he will go again. So, if Nature had not put it

into the female subconscious mind that she must fly upstream, all the Mayfly in the world would have been
washed into the sea a million years ago.

Such is the Mayfly which mainly hatches in June. But
that is not the fly's fault. During the Middle Ages the
mathematicians told the great Pope Gregory that the calendar
was getting out of time with the sun and the planets. They
persuaded him to alter the calendar by ten days – the
Gregorian calendar. England did not fall in line until the
eighteenth century when the Mayfly and Cambridge May
Week found themselves out of step, and the anniversaries
of such events as the Battle of Harfleur were falsified.

The Russians, being Orthodox and having less respect
for Popes, waited two centuries longer. No doubt in the
future another such adjustment will be needed. Perhaps
by then we shall at last be One World and can all do it on
the same day.

The Mayfly is an example but all the other chalk-stream
creatures have their own lives, and some of them even
more bizarre. I was guided into an understanding of them
by the Air Chief Marshal. I've no idea how he distinguished
himself in the R.A.F. but we knew him as the greatest of
the Dry Fly men.

On the train from Paddington he would sit in a first-class
carriage and tie his own flies just with his fingers – without
aid from the small fixed vice which others find essential.
As they were finished he hooked them into the lapels of
his crottle-brown Harris tweed jacket. It was the only fly-
box he ever had. When he wanted to fish with one he just
tore it out. He had done it so long that his fishing coat
appeared to have a fur collar.

Passionate in his pursuit of understanding he was always
dissatisfied with what he knew. Once after a discussion

about which flies lived on the Lambourne stream, he went out and bought a huge butterfly net. Soon he began to leave his rod behind and pursued flies instead of fish. His pockets clinked with little bottles half-filled with formalin. His collection of water-flies of all species, both sexes and each life stage ended in the British Museum.

Quiet in voice and gentle in manners, he looked such a ragamuffin when dressed for fishing that sometimes an Inspector would spot him from the corridor and slide over the First-class to ask him for his ticket. Apologetically – as if he didn't want to embarrass the man – he would present the gold medallion that entitled a very few of the great to free railway travel.

The Colonel was neither quiet-voiced nor gently-mannered. he was something from the old days. He was arrogant, critical, irascible, class-conscious – and a dear, good friend. The keepers greatly respected him even though, if one of them questioned something he said, he would shout, 'Now then! That's enough of this Jack's-as-good-as-his-Master stuff, if you please!' Everything he thought, he said. Once when I had bought a new fishing jacket he said 'Damned if you don't look smarter fishing than when you're supposed to be tidy.' Once I took a famous journalist down to fish as a guest. He was so frightened of the Colonel that he ran away. The old boy watched him disappear and said, 'Is the feller ill? Ought we to do something?'

The first time I met him I was a beginner and wandering up and down the river looking for a decent fish. I passed him three times – an unforgivable offence on dry-fly water. On the third occasion he spoke, 'I haven't met you, Sir, but you're certainly a bloody traveller'.

'I'm sorry, but I can't find a decent fish'.

'I'm not surprised' he said. 'Sit down beside me and I'll show you five.'

Under the Colonel's tuition I learned to watch four rises a long way off and know which was the biggest fish.

He showed me all the things that can be done with a dry-fly tackle, most of which I never learned. Once I had been trying to cover a fish that rose under a hawthorn bush across the river and had lost three flies in the process. 'Allow me' he said, and as his cast extended he shot a bit of line and wiggled the rod-tip. The fly swung round in a curve to the right and slid under the fish from above.

The trout ignored it. 'Now he's done for' I thought. But he flourished his rod like a Japanese ribbon-dancer, brought the fly out again from above and kept his line alive.

'Um' he said. 'A somewhat complicated recovery!' Then he made the same cast again and caught him.

He fancied himself as a chef and once, when a swan hit the power-lines and fell dead at our feet, he invited us all to a swan dinner on Sunday night. It was quite horrible.

Dry-fly fishing is like chess – however long you live you cannot master it. It has been wonderful, but I know that old as I am I may myself outlive it. The sport is in decay, and won't last much longer.

The landowners who thought of the streams just as one of the pleasures of their landscape have been taught to maximise their inputs. Water where once three or four people fished are now let to syndicates of twelve or fifteen rods. Where five or six fish a week were caught, it must now be twenty-five if all the newcomers are to get their money's worth. So farmed fish have to be stocked in increasing numbers and increasingly these are 'rainbows' the fast-growing restaurant fish that rise without discretion and cannot breed in the wild. The Colonel called them 'bloody freshwater mackerel'.

More serious still, the chalk-streams themselves are threatened. If you build an atomic plant on the downland you can push borings down into the chalk that will extract the water right on the spot for cooling, after which it blows away upwind as steam. Also, the water authorities now bore the chalk and rob the springs before the water has entered the stream. Thus they get perfectly clean water that needs no cleaning and filtration. Very cost-effective!

The first stream in which I caught a chalk-stream trout was robbed of its life some years ago. One stream I now fish is robbed at its springs to take water for Bournemouth. Bournemouth is where its going to anyway! Several of the most famous trout rivers now stay alive only on rations of water obtained from the authorities through interminable legal wrangling.

And then there's farming. In the war they dredged the streams to dry up their grandfathers' meads and grow corn. Now most of the hatches have been removed and while in the rainy time the farmers demand the land be kept clear of floods, in growing time they claim irrigation licenses to take water again from the shrunken summer streams.

The land that was water-meadows began to know the new insecticides and herbicides. Then came agriculture's two most up-to-date pollutions. Dairy slurry and silage-liquor now kills more fish than factory pollution used to do. A man who destroys fifteen thousand fish invites a fine that can be covered by a third of the cost of a three-year old secondhand tractor which, in any case, has been written off the balance-sheet.

That's the way it is. But who are we whose pleasure should stand in the way of progress? The cooling of atomic

stations. The pressure washing of roadliners. The shower-
ing of the millions. Or the balance-sheets of an overproduc-
tive, subsidised agriculture.

After all the millions of years through which nature prepared its perfect environment, it seems that Dry Fly fishing
is to be enjoyed for no more than a century and a half.

It was lovely while it lasted. I was once able to show it
to Uncle Stanley before he died. He had never seen a chalk
stream and came down to fish on one for a fortnight in
June. This time it was he who asked a thousand questions.

As he left I said 'What do you think of it, Uncle?'

'Ee Ummer!' he said – perhaps the first time that Yorkshire
ejaculation had been heard in the chalk valleys. 'Ee
Ummer!' he said 'I'd like to be your age! And stopping
round here!'

5
Good for a Feed

I am sure that when our earliest antecedents roamed the unchanged wilderness – in the days when all food was free – and spoke in a language of perhaps fifty words, that two of those words were 'good' and 'feed'. I imagine a little country boy – in the days when they were all country boys – trotting ahead of the family group and coming upon a place where the berries grew thick. I see him running back to the rest pointing over his shoulder and shouting, 'Good for a Feed!'

Last week an elderly neighbour looked into the pen where two of my Black Game cockerels were tucking into some rolled barley. He grunted his approval and said, 'They'll be good for a feed.'

The idea of 'Food for Free' still has a fascination for many. You can buy expensive books by men who roam the landscape in trainers and plastic cagoules that will tell you how to cook nettles, gather chanterelles or bake a hedgehog in the way that the gipsies are supposed to do.

A lifetime ago, when we were living what might now be called a peasant life, we already had a thousand years experience of doing better than that; of stuffing home-grown corn of a select strain into the vastly improved descendants of the jungle fowl, of roasting the potato that was brought from the Andes, boiling the sprouts that came from Belgium, pruning pears of a variety developed in France, making butter from cows that in one lactation gave enough milk for fifty wild calves. Time had already produced a wealth of new things that were good for a feed.

So we didn't take a lot from the wild. As I have said, we ate none of the coarse fish that Uncle and I caught in such numbers; but we did take them home in a wet sack. They were good protein and we boiled them up in a copper and mashed them up for pig and chicken feed. In the First War particularly, many cottagers kept their chickens in lay only by dint of coarse-angling. In time of rationing an egg is an egg, even if it tastes faintly fishy.

I should allay the fears of conscientious club anglers by saying that, in those days before the keep-net, the fish continued to burgeon in the water. They were there in much larger numbers than now, and grew to a bigger average weight. Of course, the rivers ran full and clear and were rich in feed. There were no slurry tanks or silage pits, nor flushes of surplus nitrogen. And there were not three and a half million anglers.

Of course people have always made the best of a bad job. The fact is that almost all the coarse fish in Britain belong to the carp family and all of them are pretty awful on a plate. The monks had fish-ponds full of carp and ate them once a week for the sake of the protein. Isaac Walton was generous with his recipes but each of them has innumerable flavourings added. Anyway, Walton has long been suspected to be something of a phoney, and his statement that the chub cooked for him by the landlady was delicious seems to settle it. The received definition of cooked chub is well-known – 'Wet cotton-wool full of pins.'

The pike, which is not of the carp clan, is still cooked in France, but by a method which is significant. The fish is first stewed in a long kettle. The flesh is then taken from the skeleton and the flakes of it separated from the hundreds of small Y-shaped bones with which they are infested. Then it is pounded in a mortar until it is no more than a fish cream which is shaped in 'quennelles' – a sort of rissole – to which all kinds of herbal and other tastes can be added. The French are masters of flavouring. One is reminded of the claim that a good French sauce chef can make 'escargots' from pieces of Michelin tyre.

The superiority of sea-fish was known from the beginning to country people close to the coast. I think that those who liked to live well took care to settle in such places; like the Cistercian monks at Beaulieu where the estuary is still seine-netted by the locals as it was by them. Early on the packers brought the produce of the smoke-houses – kippers, bloaters and smoked haddock – into the interior.

The rich could always look after themselves. In an outbuilding up at our local big house there hung the remains of two long hazel baskets, apparently once roped together at the top. They were referred to as the oyster baskets.

It was the Squire's custom to set up a chain of horsemen across the countryside – a sort of oyster pony post – all the way to the coast. Over hill and dale the oysters were rushed across the country, being flung from one saddle to the next, to arrive fresh for a banquet at the Manor.

I always wished I could have been one of those gallopers. I'm sure they were the hunt servants and other country lads who knew the lie of the land, and that they would have taken a line straight across country. In those days the lanes would have been impassable most of the time when there was an R in the month.

When McAdam improved the roads they began to build fast-wheeled vehicles and then with the coming of the early railways it was possible to get sea-fish to just about anywhere that people wanted it. And that was everywhere.

We had a high-speed fishman, a third generation specialist.

His name was Luke Howe. He had a high-wheeled flatcart and a little half-bred Hackney pony called Bobby. They covered the ground faster than any other turn-out in the district to the jingling of harness bells. When we were little, and full of what we thought were comic jokes, we used to listen for Luke coming down the lane. As he brought Bobby round the bends like a rally-driver we used to cry 'Luke Howe he goes', and then fall about laughing. He must have got very tired of that joke but he never showed any sign of having heard it. In fact, Luke hardly ever spoke. He would stand there while you picked what you wanted off the flatcart, then mention the price, take the money, hop up like a little monkey and be away.

Over at the coast where the boats came into the fish-market just about daybreak, they would load a box for Luke onto the earliest train and he would pick it up at our nearest station to be on his way before anyone had finished breakfast. He sat on the front edge of the flatcart from which a sack-full of straw hung down into which he thrust his legs on cold mornings. For twenty seven miles he sat with his head stuck forward and his eyes fixed on Bobby's ears – like a high-speed roach fisherman. They did that trip together, with variations of routes round the hamlets, for twenty-five years. This was the second pony he'd had since he started the job at the age of thirteen and Bobby took the job on at the age of four. Luke fed him full of oats and he trotted – fit as a trained racehorse – for twenty-five years.

The mystery about Luke was where he put his money. At the end of his round he emptied his pocket on to the bar to buy a pint and there'd never be more than a shilling. Some of the boys went over his cart while Bobby was munching out the back, but they didn't find any secret drawers or anything. He would have made a great smuggler. My own theory was that it went in the pad of the pony harness. The bells would disguise the jingle.

Luke didn't talk in the pub either. He just sat there, knees together and hands together, looking straight over his beer. You could have guessed he was a long distance pony driver. Just as you tell the ploughman with his boots going clink-clonk-clink-clonk on the flagstone floor – one foot in the ridge and one in the furrow. Or the cowman, with a right ear like a red cabbage and his cap over the left one. Or the carter with his yorks above his knees and an obvious belief that he was the best man in the place.

Thus we got the sea-fish, and none fresher. There was however, one creature that was exempted from our distaste for the freshwater species: the eel. Everyone knows how good eels are. It is the otter's favourite dish. A heron prefers an eel to a trout – and so, I think, do I. It's true that the eel is something of a scavenger – but so is a lobster.

If you fish for an eel with a dead minnow he'll come to it from a long way off. Of course, a fish cannot smell in the water but they have an equivalent talent with which the eel is best of all endowed – the ability to catch the faintest trace of a taste in the water. Uncle and I once caused this to be perfectly demonstrated. Up at the top of the shallow below the mill bridge, where just three inches of water runs down over yards of clean gravel we placed a small, dead fish. It lay there while we sat motionless against the bushes. Half an hour before dusk an eel appeared at the bottom of the stickle, swinging from side to side like a pointer dog. He quartered the gravel in narrowing sweeps and brought himself straight to his dinner.

We had eels everywhere. Apart from the river they were in the farm-ponds and in the meres – often far from anywhere. But nobody ever saw any sign of them breeding. In ancient times this mystery was solved by the usual method of inventing a magical belief. Eels, they said, grew from stray horse hairs that fell in the water.

The truth was discovered by a Danish deep-sea naturalist in the time of my childhood. All our eels breed in the deep ocean off Central America. Once they have fed themselves big and green and fat they suddenly turn silver, make off down the river and set out for the West Indies. As to why they would endure such a laborious journey, I think I know the answer. Because it is built so differently from other fish the eel does not have muscles capable of squeezing out the spawn. Only in the warm depths of the Saragasso Sea can it comfortably descend deep enough for the water pressure to do the job for it. It also knows – or Nature knows – that from that district of the ocean runs a current that will bring the little eels to Europe were they can ascend the rivers and spread themselves so conveniently over our countryside.

But how do they do it? How do they find their way to distant lakes in no way connected with the river? Eels travel quite easily across land if there is rain to keep them wet. This I know to be true because I have seen them. When out in the dark rabbiting with the night lamp I have several times been aware of a movement and, turning the lamp on it, seen eels hurrying across wet fields like grass snakes out jogging.

Apart from fishing for them with a dead minnow I have a more rewarding method of catching eels that I learned from a gipsy. I kept the secret for thirty years and then finally divulged it to a lady for reasons of wartime necessity, and also perhaps of sentimentality. She had three children and when I stayed with them on leave I found that the ration books made it a very tight thing. I went off in the night and the next day we all had a feast of jellied eels.

You start with a big loose-woven corn sack and into the mouth of it you sew a foot-wide ring twisted from hazel rod. Three strings are tied to the ring which meet together two feet up and join a single line about forty feet long. Into the bottom you put a brick and then an armful of straw. On top of this you put the bait – rabbit guts, for instance, or a high kipper, and another armful of straw on top.

At sunset you tie the end of the line to a tree-root, coil it all carefully on the ground, and then whirl the sack around your head and hurl it into the water, preferably in a deepish place between two beds of weed.

At first light you pick up the string again and just with your fingertips ease all the slack out of it without the slightest jerk. Now run back up the bank and drag the sack out. The feeding eels will be found tangled in the straw. If you have done it right – and particularly if there has been a touch of thunder in the air – you should have several pounds.

After I was abroad again my lady-friend went into business. She made herself five sets of the equipment and worked them nightly around the big ornamental lake nearby. The local rabbiting-man had a share of the catch for supplying the bait, and for two years she supplied her rationed neighbours. But then the American Army took over the big house and hosed down their vehicles in the shallow end of the lake. The motor-oil and the film of diesel that spread over the surface reduced that abundant lake to a dead pit.

Years later I was talking in America of my home countryside when a man said 'I know that place. I was stationed at the Castle'.

'In that case', I said (I hope without rancour) 'You have a good deal to answer for'.

There may be some difference of opinion about jellied eels; there can be none when eels are smoked.

We smoked eels in a wooden barrel with the ends taken out. We built a fire on the ground and when it had died to a hot glow covered it with a couple of buckets of oak sawdust from Harry Brandon's sawpit. On top of this stood the barrel with an old wooden copper lid on top. The eels were split open and hung on sticks that ran across near the top. With a few holes down at the bottom, controlled by spiles, and a few little wedges to tilt the lid, we adjusted it to get the slowest draught that would not die. Against hot or cold smoked eels I promise you smoked salmon is nowhere.

Again it was at first light that we went to seek the tastiest of all wild delicacies, the Field Mushroom. You have to have a feel for mushrooms and you can tell by the warmth of the night and the feel of the air when they will come in quantity – born in the dawn and good for just a day. Unless you were smart the tramps would be ahead of you; and the gipsies and just about everybody because – in respect of the mushroom – the ancient feeling for food that just has to be gathered was at its strongest. The old methods of grazing and muck-spreading kept them coming. Mushrooms would turn up everywhere and with them people who in ordinary days would never leave the footpaths and in other seasons were soundly asleep at daybreak. To some farmers it felt like 'The Day of the Tryffids'. Some broke up a block of mushroom spawn, spread it about a bit and put up notices that said 'Private – Cultivated Mushrooms'.

The Old Man was very generous about people mushroom-picking, but we were away from any centre of population

and shared a native link with those around us. None who
came would leave without dropping some of their pickings
in our back-kitchen, and probably getting breakfast for
their trouble. We needn't have gone out ourselves except
for the fun.

Mother used to sort them into three. The ones just open
flat for prime eating. Those born a few hours earlier that
had flattened into soft plates for mushroom soup. The
buttons which were short of flavour she strung through
with a needle and thread and hung up to dry. They opened
a bit as they did so and were used for winter flavouring.

Modern farming has made the field mushroom comparatively rare. How can it matter when the mushroom farmers
are sending millions to the supermarkets – all unblemished
and sorted for size. Sorry the man who can't taste the
difference! A mushroom farmer said to me, 'I don't know
what you're on about. It's just the same thing.' 'It is not
the same thing' said the great Doctor Manners, Professor
of Mycology, who used to take me on fungus hunts. 'It's
a different species. The Field Mushroom is Agaricus Cam-
pestris and the commerical mushroom is Agaricus Bisporus.'
So they can put that in the Trade Descriptions Act.

One interesting question about food from the wild is
why we do not eat squirrels, and – more extraordinarily
still – why we have forgotten that we used to eat them in
large quantities. In 1837 it was estimated that twenty
thousand red squirrels a year were sold, chiefly at Newgate
and Leadenhall Markets, and that they were considered a
delicacy. Yet Dickens who was writing at that time, and
whose books contain mention of scores of things eaten,
makes no mention of them. Not even the oldest cookbooks
have recipes.

They were taken up by the night waggoners and, from

the Home Counties, would arrive quite fresh. It is thought, for instance, that bunches of fifty or sixty a day came to the capital from the New Forest.

In the Forest they were hunted with throwing sticks – the oldest weapon known to man for the pursuit of small game. No doubt in earliest days they collected every stone with a hole into which a stick could be pushed for a handle. I have met old country people who still think a stone with a hole in it is lucky, and will put a string through and hang it to the eaves of the house to bring good fortune. But the knobs that I have found lying below old trees in the forest have been of lead, about the size of a bantam's egg, with a three-eighth inch hole to take the handle. The squirrel hunter carried a shoulder-bag full – like a quiver of arrows – and it was easy enough to lose them in the long grass.

I have tried my hand at it. I found that a foot-long piece of hazel rod was right for a handle and yoghurt cups up on a branch make suitable squirrels. I found myself improving quite fast and I am sure that if I had started small I could have been a squirrel hunter. One of my dogs had an instinct for it. He watched politely as long as I missed but, when the yoghurt cup was knocked out of the tree, he was on it in a minute.

The Americans do have squirrel recipes in their cookbooks. They love eating their grey squirrel, which is now our squirrel, and they have trained squirrel dogs. But we didn't eat them even when we had a food shortage. In fact, in war time there was a scheme for getting rid of squirrels as pests that threatened the food supply. If you took their tails along to the man from the Min. of Ag. he would give you a shilling each for them. He didn't want the bodies. This gave another opportunity to the children of my lady-friend. They made a number of squirrel-traps –

you can do it with four foot of wire netting – and kept them baited with acorns. They claimed the money for the tails and sold the rest at the nearby US Air Force Base.

The most widely gathered of all the wild harvests was the blackberry. In the Old Country this was regarded as women's work, not for reasons to which the new women would now take neurotic objection but because they came mostly at harvest time, and harvest mattered most of all. So the hedgerows and the lanes were full of the little groups beloved of Edwardian water-colourists – a woman in straw hat and apron, carrying grandfather's walking stick by the bottom end, two or three toddlers in pinnies and a baby in a pram that was piled up with baskets.

Mother could do wonders with blackberries. Gardeners have never produced a fruit that tastes better. Nowadays I grow them on wires in the garden and prune them with great care. So many noxious sprays drift into the hedges, and those gathered in the lanes now have been covered with diesel mist from the many tractors and then coated with the fine dust that comes up from the wheels.

There have been other wild foods that have gone the other way – from domestication into the wild. The Romans in Britain kept cages full of the edible dormouse which now lives wild in just one or two places. The Fallow Deer arrived first to the walled, parkland meadows of the Barons. The rabbit was brought from the Mediterranean and lived for at least two centuries in protected warrens until it became hardy enough to take to our open countryside.

In any case the rabbit is legally ground game. All game has always, at law, belonged to somebody – usually the person on whose land it is. It is not to be obtained by gathering but by poaching. And that is another subject.

Snipe, the Old Man's bird.

Corncrake, yesterday's bird.

150 years of fishing: (from top left to bottom right) 1857, 1913, 1938, 1988.

Hay time, the rick builders.

Butcher, fast delivery service.

German bear-leaders, England 1913.

The wandering umbrella man.

Heavy horses, when man depended on them.

The woodman, the winter cropping of the woods.

An Old Man's Turn-out.

The best view in the world.

Bringing the past back to life.

6

A Shining Night

There's more than one man in Australia who sits now in comfort on his limitless sheep-station because one night his great-great-grandfather looked out of the door after supper and said 'Tis a shining night'. Then he took down from under the cottage eaves a long pole in two pieces that could be scarfed together with a leather bootlace, and had one of his old lady's darning needles fixed in the top end.

The reason why this occasion should have been fateful for him and his descendants is complicated – like most things concerned with poaching. For the moment, suffice it to explain why he should have been interested in 'a shining night' in the season of the year.

Sometimes it happens that when the moon is bright the land is covered by a veil of misty cloud. The light from above makes the mist shine like lighted ground glass. When you look up through the trees on such a night everything is silhouetted against the silver screen – in particular the roosting pheasants.

In the big trees they will be sitting too high but in the copses and the willow spinnies they will be just the right height for the pole. You use it exactly like a billiard cue. Reaching up high with your left hand to make a bridge you work the needle to within four inches of the breast. Then cue cleanly with plenty of follow through and, pierced to the heart, the pheasant falls without a flutter.

So quietly can the job be done by the experienced

reprobate that he will probably also take the other bird that was sitting next to it.

However successful he was he would go home empty-handed. The sack of birds would be found by Old Glory, the drover on his way to market, hanging out of fox-reach in the hedge and marked by three stones set at the roadside. After a journey under the straw in the market float the birds would reach the poulterer, or perhaps be dumped in the stables of the respectable Crown Hotel which had a taproom frequented by the drovers.

The poacher wouldn't want to take pheasants home; first because he would be sure to leave feathers lying about; and second because he didn't think they were much good to eat. He would rather have a hare. A hare would feed a family twice over with good, strong meat; and a hare's skin could be burned in one piece. That is, after the scalp and the ears had been cut off for the Vicar who tied his own trout-flies. The Vicar, who was noticeably righteous in most respects, was to be trusted in the matter of poaching; in fact he once hobbled home from a day of invited trout-fishing with a salmon down his waders, complaining that he had sprained his ankle.

Beyond all that, if a keeper caught a man with pheasants His Lordship would insist on prosecution, while he might look more kindly on a hard-working farmworker who went home with a hare.

There are many subtleties in the sociology of poaching. The relations between the haves and have-nots have varied a lot in the course of its history.

In the beginning there were the Forests and the Chases. The former were the hunting-grounds of the King – the Forest of Dean, Forest of Arden, Sherwood Forest, the New Forest, added to the many others by William the Conqueror.

They had the serious practical purpose of supplying meat for the Monarch and his Court, his Officials and his Army, when they were in progress around the country in days before refrigeration. Similar hunting grounds of the great nobles, in their own districts, were called 'Chases'. In these places the mighty reserved to themselves what were called the 'Beasts of the Chase' – Deer, Wild Boar, and the Hare, the substantial meat-providers.

Preserving these animals from poaching over such large areas was difficult so they turned to the use of savage penalties. In the Royal Forests ordinary people lived not under the common law of England but under the Royal Forest Law which in earlier times provided for death and maiming. It is said that in the New Forest a man was once blinded for spying on the King's deer. Even the dogs were not immune. A yokel's dog kept in the Forest that was big enough to hunt deer had toes cut off to slow him down.

Apart from the Beasts of the Chase, an ordinary man was pretty free to seek food. As far as birds were concerned the gentry pursued them by falconry and there is a strong impression that they did this chiefly for delight in the art and were just as happy if the hawk struck a rook or a heron as a good dinner.

Among ordinary men there were those who followed the trade of 'fowler'.

I must admit that, in the days when humans were fewer and birds far more numerous, I should like to have been apprenticed to the craft of fowler. It must have had all the fascination of bird-watching, together with the satisfaction of exercising a dozen different and intricate skills of working with nets and traps and snares and springes; of making decoys, mixing bird-lime to secret recipes and whittling bird-calls to exactly the right note. And of wandering alone over the countryside as your own master.

On the shore they hung flight nets at just the right height to catch the duck that would later skim just over the high-tide line. I saw this done many years ago by the last practitioner of it, out on the muds of the Wash. Now flight-nets, which were also set in the forest glades to catch the circling woodcock, are used only under licence to catch wild birds for marking.

Over the wide fields they captured skylarks because the rich would pay well to have a dish of larks' tongues. They did this with the aid of an extraordinary implement called a 'twirler'. A cross-piece of wood was set on a peg stuck in the ground and made to spin round by pulling a long string wound round its axle. I have one of these. It is beautifully made of ebony and the top edge is carved to a perfect curve along the edge of which little pieces of mirror are inlaid. You can see that on a bright day the spinning 'twirler' would reflect the sun in sparkles of light up into a wide circle of the sky above. When a soaring skylark saw it he flew down to it.

Why did he fly down to it? It is my theory that the skylark, endlessly singing above his territory on a summer day, would frequently need a drink; as would anyone who sang his heart out for hours on end. To him, I think, the little glitter of the twirler meant a puddle. And that's why he flew down to it.

You may still find in a country pub somewhere an ancient who will talk with relish about the days of 'sparrow-pie'. This really means 'little bird pie'. When protein was short large numbers of little birds were eaten and they were not particular about the species. Dozens of them would be boiled until their flesh could be picked off and made into a pie. Long ago when we moved to our first farm there stood in the corner of the barn an old clap-net. Two very long poles were tied together at their thin tips so that, if you held the butts under your arms, they formed themselves into an arch. This arch was covered with a thin soft net of cotton. In the dusk of evening this was lightly beaten against the ivy of the house, the high hedges and the sides of the hay and corn-ricks. As soon as there came a flutter the net was closed by 'clapping' the two poles together.

When Pointers first came up from Spain their job was to find and put up birds for the falcon that was hovering above, but the Setter was the servant of the fowler. He developed his peculiar crouching habit for the purpose of netting partridges.

The partridge, when it senses danger, will always take refuge in concealment before flight. The whole covey – that is the partridge family – will crouch close together in the long grass, silent and unmovable. It is known as 'jukking' and nothing will make them juk tighter than the sight of a hawk in the sky. In the earliest writings on the fowler's art there are instructions for making a kite in the shape of a falcon. When setting out to net the birds the kite was flown overhead to stop the birds from moving.

The setting dog would quarter the ground with the wind in his face, moving to and fro until he caught the scent of the hidden covey. Once he had it he would move stealthily forward. The fowler and his mate followed with a twenty foot square net, carefully folded. When the dog knew he was within four or five feet of the birds he would sink down to the ground and crouch with his nose pointing to them. The net would be delicately spread and the two men, one on each front corner, would slip it right over the dog's back and drop it over the whole partridge family.

People who keep Setters today – and even win with them

at Crufts – can scarcely imagine the thrill of working with them. Once 'set' to a close scent a good dog would not move a muscle until the job was done. There is an old story about fowlers who were working in the late evening when a mist rolled down the hill. They lost sight of the dog who was well ahead of them. After searching and calling in vain they went home. At daybreak the mist had cleared and they found the dog, still setting a scent that he had found the night before. They caught a covey of birds which had squatted while the dog held them for eight or nine hours! A likely tale! But you don't have to believe it to understand that admiration for the dog caused it to be told.

I'm sure there is not a setter alive today that has a net pulled over his back. In any case it is unthinkable that the many arts of the fowler should be performed today. Still, to understand the problems of modern conservation, it is well to remember that seventy years ago when I was little birds of all kinds existed abundantly around us – after centuries of fowling. Despite the twirler, the skylarks sang in the sky all day over fields where they are now unknown. Every evening we heard the Grey Partridge cocks calling the coveys to rest on land from which herbicides have removed the weed seeds on which they relied; and insecticides have robbed them of the insects on which their chicks were reared. In winter the small birds flew in clouds around the rickyard; but yesterday I read in our Country Bird Report that the sparrow must now be regarded as uncommon.

The art of fowling faded after the Battle of Waterloo as the percussion shotgun spread across the country, a weapon that would detonate a cloud of shot fast enough for feathered game to be shot on the wing. Instead of hawks and nets it was now the shooting – men who went out with pointers and setters – including Mr Pickwick. And soon the privileged among them found a way of shooting in which somebody else did the walking.

As so often in English history a new set of people assumed the role of country gentlemen. They moved in with East Indian spoils, Admiralty prize-money, the profits of coal, sugar and iron, and the fruits of banking. Land was no longer to have the monopoly of riches and power and with but a modest estate you could – by following the new fashion of driven-game shooting – put up a show of being a shooting host.

It meant rearing game birds by the thousand, and crowding them into the coverts in numbers for which Nature could never provide. It meant keeping the locals off your land and closing the footpaths which their ancestors had walked. It brought an obsession with trespass that developed over the years into a malady which the Old Man used to call 'Landowners' Disease'. Kipling is said to have been most seriously afflicted. On his small Sussex estate he sat at a top window with field-glasses, scanning his boundaries in fear of invasion, yet hoping that someone might cross the border who could be prosecuted.

But it also meant that a man need no longer walk hard all day in company with a yokel and two dogs in order to bring home three or four brace of birds. He could invite a dozen of the elite and influential to stand fifteen yards apart while the birds were driven over their heads. And he could have them all roistering at his lunch table while the Head Keeper sat outside, growling at his pocket watch and cancelling one after another of the afternoon drives. His work was to be judged by the hundreds of birds shot – and also by the scores of wild creatures, said to be

competitive in the game environment, that he himself killed
and hung on gibbets for his employer to see.

This time of new riches in the country houses brought
hardship to the rural poor. And since the yokels were
needed on shooting days to beat the woods and put the
birds over the line, they became aware of the vast numbers
of quarry, and more familiar with their habits than those
who stood to receive them. It was quite natural that the
fashion for driven game gave birth to the great age of
poaching. Within fifty years two generations of country
lads had grown up knowing every trick of the game, and
taking a pleasure in it that amounted to ecstasy. 'It's my
delight on a shining night in the season of the year'.

The cleverest dog was now the poacher's dog – though
he usually looked just a little ragamuffin. The pointers and
setters died gradually away, to be replaced by the fetch-
and-carry retrievers that 'Stonehenge' – writing in *The Field*
in the eighteen-fifties called 'Servants Hall Dogs'.

While the poacher worked his dog would crouch on
watch and if he noticed the sound or smell of anyone else
he would creep up to his master and, in the dark, touch
his hand with a cold nose. When the man with the needle-
pole wanted a hare for his own pot he would go out with
a gate-net inside his trousers – a soft, wide-meshed net
about the size of a single bedspread. This he hung loosely
in a gateway or a hedge-gap on any one of the hare's
habitual routes that he knew by heart. Then he lit his pipe
and walked on. His dog would slip through the hedge and
quarter the field until the hare was put up and then drive
it – sheep-dog fashion – into the net. Having killed it there
he would return to walk respectably at heel. The hare could
be fetched when the coast was clear.

One of the satisfactory things about poaching was that it

did not involve guilt. No poacher ever thought of himself as a criminal. Of course, if you were caught you would be in trouble. But it wasn't fair to the village Bobby to get caught. It was embarrassing for him. Even the keepers would turn a blind eye. They were, on the whole, contemptuous of their masters. But you shouldn't put your trust in that. The Old Man used to say – 'If the keeper lets you take a hare you'll never finish paying for it.'

Poachers were hard to catch up with – except for the gangs that came from the towns and openly challenged the keepers to violent encounters. The standard of skill of the country poachers was very high inded. Why, then, did the night when Great-Grandfather went out with his needle-pole turn out so fatefully?

The outcome of it was decided on the other side of the world. Australia had been used as a place to send the 'criminal classes' and, now the time had come to open up and develop the country, the Governor General said it could not be done with his work-gangs of thieves and pickpockets. Now he needed good men who could move out into the country.

So the word went from Westminster to the Lords-Lieutenant and from them to the squires who were magistrates. The search was on for good men who could be caught poaching.

Great-Grandfather could milk and plough and thatch and like most farm-hands had a dozen different rural skills. The day he was taken – on information extracted from the drover – was his last free day in his native land. On the ship he joined hundreds of others swept up in the same cynical operation. It was a bad day for the man but perhaps a very good one for his descendants. I hope that their sheep-station may be called 'Needlepole'.

7
Life after Death

In the county of Dorset, to which life finally led me, there are the remains of a hundred and fifteen dead villages. Some of them have left hardly a trace, though when the land is newly ploughed there can be seen a pattern of broken bits of pottery, with sometimes the bowl of a clay pipe or a belt buckle. Once the badgers dug up a cut-throat razor that proved to be Jacobean.

Elsewhere you may see a few green humps and in the hedges the degraded descendants of apple trees. People say 'There used to be a village, here, but everybody died in the Black Death.' They like simple explanations.

It is true that the pestilence started here. Just as it is now believed that AIDS was taken to the USA from Africa by one blonde Scandinavian airline steward, so it seems that one army supply-ship brought the Black Death to Britain.

Having travelled from China along the Old Silk Road the disease was established in 1345 in Constantinople. From there it went west with Mediterranean shipping. Greece in 1346. Spain in 1347. From there it was probably taken over the Pyrenees by marauding Moors to Picardy where the English army was fighting. A returning supply-ship landed at its home-port of Melcombe Regis (Weymouth) in the spring of 1348. By autumn the Black Death had reached London.

Of course, the Dorset people of the fourteenth century lived solitary and superstitious lives. Most of them never travelled more than fifteen miles, let alone down to the coast. So they preferred a theory of their own – the plague was being carried across the world by an evil south wind. Until quite recently I am told you could find in Dorset old houses facing northwards, with blank windowless walls on the south side. Houses built with their backs to the plague.

It is now believed that more than 40% of the people in Europe died in the Black Death. The evidence is sketchy but in the town of Avignon, where the papacy kept records, the population fell from over thirty thousand to less than nine.

Such a loss could have left a hundred and fifteen Dorset villages empty. But if you mark all the villages in question on the map it is clear that the story is not so simple. Of the hundred and fifteen dead places about eighty were on the high chalk, only the remaining few were on the clay and heathland that cover most of the county.

Why should the Black Death travel over the chalk in preference to the more populous lower places? It seems clear that history must offer a less tabloid explanation and – in search of an understanding of the countryside – it is worthwhile tracing the history of our inhabited places.

There is no better place for imagining how life began for us here in Britain than the window at which I sit. There, to the south, stretches for twenty miles a great clay vale, cut into fields on average less than half the size of those that belong to modern agriculture. Only here or there are they ploughed, where a streak of green land relieves the heavy soil. Between them are hedges, in which the oak trees stand, and along which miles of ditch water brooks make a tortuous way to drain into the River Stour. The boundaries of this – Hardy's 'Vale of the little dairies' – are marked by a sweeping half-circle of chalk hills. Sometimes they are cloaked in mist. Sometimes they shine in the sun while the vale remains dank and misty. They seem to form a weather frontier. Once – perhaps twice, at times ages apart – they were the frontier to the sea when it covered the vale. Along the bottom edge of the hills, if you dig for it, you can find a shingle beach. In the walls of some of the oldest cottages are giant fossil sea-shells, valued maybe for magical reasons in superstitious times. As the sea fell back the whole vale became a bog-forest of oak. At just one point there is a gap in the hills through which the river carries the waters on their present way to the sea.

The Ancient British saw this view exactly the other way round. The bog-forest was impassable and dangerous. It was a land of bears and wild oxen, wolves and wild-cats. The river was dammed by the beaver. Men lived on the dry chalk tops among thickets of thorns. They scratched at the light soil with deer antlers and scraped away at sticks and hides with sharpened flints. They wandered endlessly over a skeleton of high chalk land running from the Purbecks to Beachy Head and up to the Wash. They left no houses behind because they probably made brushwood huts at camping sites, only the remains of the embanked forts into which they fled for safety, and the mounds under which they buried their dead. They left no literature, only a few words that are preserved in the Welsh and Gaelic tongues. On the top of the hills I see are valleys that are still called 'coombs'.

It was left to later tribes – the Belgae from Gaul and the various Saxon tribes from Baltic Europe – to clear the lower ground. They had iron axes and ploughs. They could cut down trees and cultivate heavy land. They penetrated the impassable lowlands by way of the rivers, clearing the forest on either bank, building their villages at the places where the river could be forded.

So there came into existence two lands looking up and down at one another. On the hills the people whom the Romans had called Britons. Below, under the Germanic name of England, those who were founding the prosperous farming of the future.

In the tribal struggles of these centuries chieftains became petty kings who in turn overcame one another and were themselves forced into allegiance until there grew the 'feudal' system – the duty system in which every man was subject to his master from the serf up to the King himself.

That system was intact – though admittedly getting old and a bit shaky – when the fateful ship sailed home from Picardy. In bringing the plague it brought a revolution. The Black Death was a phoenix fire out of which arose the English countryside as we know it, and the English country people as we think of them.

Suddenly there was a shortage of labour. The feudal Lords found work undone, and their own power of men loosening. Men who had never been allowed to leave their place of birth could wander off to another estate and be welcomed, rather than being sent back like a runaway slave. And a man could now negotiate his own reward. Wage bargaining was born in 1348.

Further, there was land set free. On the outskirts of the under-manned estates men began to achieve holdings of their own. It was this that brought the people down from the poorer hill-tops. It was not, in some way, the plague selectively killing the inhabitants of the chalk settlements. They themselves abandoned them and came down at last to the fat land below. They had looked down in envy ever since Iron Age axes cleared the forest. Now their time had come. At last there was room for everybody.

Of course, the land itself still belonged to the powerful, but there were granted 'life-holdings', 'copy holdings' and other systems that allowed a man to work land on his own behalf. This is how 'cottages' were born. A 'cotter' was one who had been allowed to clear a new holding in the baronial waste and woodland which was called his 'cottage'. Even now small country people rarely speak of a dwelling as a cottage. However small it is they usually speak of it as a house.

At the same time men who had been bound to the land by birth found freedom to venture into crafts and trade; and people whose place had been fixed to one spot could travel the country. Drovers, thatchers, turners and masons. Waggoners, tinkers, basket-makers, saddlers and brewers. They could choose their own places, find their own customers, make their own bargains and do things their own way. The life that we were to inherit had been born out of death.

Of the lives of ordinary people before this great change almost nothing is to be seen or read. It had been a life of drudgery and submission. I long ago realised that I could hear in the ancient English of the Bible a phrase which, without reference to religion, they must have repeated often – 'Grant me, O Lord'. 'Grant me, O Lord, that I may cut firewood; that my daughter may marry; that I may have a day to thatch my hut'.

They lived in hovels that soon rotted into the ground, and the buildings we know from those feudal centuries are castles, churches and manor-houses. But now they began to build small houses that their children could inherit. Fourteenth century and fifteenth century are the claims that are made on behalf of the earliest ordinary dwellings that still exist in our villages. And in that period we begin to read about the lives of people without titles or power.

Geoffrey Chaucer was a little boy learning to read and write when the fateful ship sailed into Melcombe Regis.

These early houses are now regarded by us as precious. They are listed. A friend of ours who lives in one is not allowed to put double-glazing in it – even though when it was built it had no windows, only wooden shutters. In a nearby village we have a sixteenth century cottage that is just six months old. It finally fell down in a gale and was rebuilt from scratch, this time on foundations. The brick-and-flint patterned walls are applied to a new double shell of hollow concrete blocks.

Larger or smaller as they may have been, these houses all posed the same big problem for the builders – the moving of heavy materials. The country roads were just an apology for roads. The one that runs in front of my house was once a main route though now it is small enough to be unclassified. You can dig down into it through four feet of succeeding layers of broken stone that were put on it winter after winter in order to keep waggons going. The heavy carts and ox-sledges tore up the unmade track. On the slopes the winter rains washed it down to produce the deep cuttings through which so many of the lanes now run. Down on the levels the road became just a bog.

Houses, therefore, were built from whatever was closest at hand. On the claylands there were many little brickyards. On chalky land there were big flints that rose from the soil and could be used rough, or knapped on the outside to give a grey oyster-shell finish. In woodland country the whole building was first framed with oak beams; and then stood there looking like a Dutch barn while it was roofed and the spaces between were filled with brickwork, or perhaps just with wattle daubed front and back with clay. In some places where wood was easiest the house frames are covered with clapboard.

Down the middle of the clay-plains which we overlook runs a seam of oolithic limestone. You can locate it exactly by the change of the houses from brick to stone – a stripe of stone houses exactly fitting the rock beneath, spreading just as wide as Edgar the quarry-man would reach in a day's journey with his cart.

Sometimes just enough stone would be fetched to bolster the corners of a house, and often enough brick was dragged up the hill to frame a flint building. I know of one village which stands at the foot of the chalk, with clay and stone within reach, where brick, flint and stone cottages are to be found in a picturesque assembly.

They say that a farmer is never bored on a journey either on road or rail. He is an expert on the meaning of landscape. When he sees a change of building material he knows what soil to expect, and what will grow on it, and how it needs to be cultivated. This is certainly true since the coming of easy mobility. In the old country I fancy that men lived all their lives in terms of the conditions they were born to – in a micro-habitat. Certainly the Old Man had his eyes opened when he bought our first car – a distinctly shaky second-hand Willis Overland.

The vehicle was a match for him in eccentricity. The fuel tank was in front behind the dashboard. Any weakness of the solder provided a steady drip of petrol onto the hot engine. Twice it caught fire and we had to bail out. Seven punctures he once mended by the roadside during one journey. And, on the same trip, three times took the carburettor apart to get rid of the little green chips of paint from the petrol cans from which it was filled. No petrol pump then, just a square stack of green cans against the wall of a smithy.

Mother loved the car. She insisted on being taken for a drive every Sunday afternoon. The Old Man thought driving for pleasure was an extravagance. He made his point by switching off the engine at the top of every hill and getting a free coast down the slope. Mother would shout at him to switch on before he lost all momentum. She drew the line at being asked to use the starting-handle.

Once, however, he loaded a dozen green cans on the rear luggage-rack and announced that he was going to Lincoln to see the work Great Uncle had done years before on the altar screen. He was leaving our place in the hands of the lads – an astonishing decision – because this was a holiday for Mother.

She said she was never going on another one. Apart from continuously switching off the 'peetrol', which is how he pronounced it, he stopped every couple of miles to lean on a gate and consider somebody else's farm. At last he would come back shaking his head, and say, 'So, that's how they do it round here'.

But however many different kinds of houses a traveller might see, in almost all the villages he would find a stone church. The people of those earlier centuries were in great awe of the Church. The Church had great temporal power and was at pains to keep up a show of it – at the expense of its parishioners. There were clerics whose full-time employment was to travel the parishes in order to sell the people pardon for their sins – for a proportion of their sins that is. The rest were left respectfully to God.

So that, while building his own humble dwelling from what he could find nearby, a man must contribute in money and labour to bring the stone up to a chalk hilltop or deep into a clay forest in order that the Church could stand in stone.

Up the slope behind our house alongside a broken line of oak trees there run the traces of a track that was called Dark Lane. There seem never to have been any dwellings on it but the traces suggest that it once suffered considerably heavy wear. It runs from the bottom lane up to the Church, taking a long road to find a slope much easier than the church-goers use.

It struck me one day that stone could have been floated down on rafts from the quarries to the Oak Ford. From there a side road sets out for our village, and Dark Lane leaves it just as you see the easiest slope up to the hill where the Church is built. A huge amount of labour. No doubt the stone was collected at the roadside and then – when the clay was hard in summer – every man and beast in the parish worked to drag it up the hill. Many sins must have been forgiven to get it there.

In the end, of course, this arrogant practice broke the power of the Holy See. It was this sale of indulgences all over Europe that paid to build St. Peters in Rome; and it was the rage of the parish priest, Martin Luther, at finding a pardoner at work among his people that led him to publish the Articles that started the Reformation.

As the prosperity that came from the freeing of individual initiative grew the small houses were improved. Holes in the roof became chimneys, and made it possible to have sleeping lofts. Shutters became windows. Dormer windows in the roof turned lofts into bedrooms and changed ladders into staircases.

As ordinary men succeeded some of the houses grew bigger – farm houses, merchants' and craftsmen's houses – filling in the gap between the Manor House and the old hovels. But the materials and styles remained localised. But finally the roads were improved, the canals were made and then we built the railways. That was the biggest change of all. You can stand in the middle of any English village and see the evidence of it. Waggon-loads of Midland brick and grey Welsh slate travelled the lines to everywhere and stood in the little railway sidings for the local builder to collect. See if you can point them out – the railway houses.

Very few who now live in the villages are country people. Modern farming doesn't need many people. If you stand in a village street at eight in the morning now you are likely to see most of the population get into their cars with briefcases. They want the cottages and the countryside to be preserved. This nostalgia is for the country life that was built by those who were freed to do things for themselves. I haven't heard anybody suggest reviving the feudal system.

8

The Eyes on the front of the Face

When I first went to America the country was under the spell of two crazy black men who spoke extemporary nonsense on the wireless at six o'clock each evening. The New York Telephone Company reported that phone-calls dropped by 40% when Moran and Mack were on the air.

On the night of my arrival I listened to them discussing the futility of getting up early to catch a worm. I was gripped. The next night they were discussing the mistakes that had been made in the design of the human body. The mouth, they thought, should have been on the top of the head – in order that when you were late for work you could put a sandwich under your hat and have breakfast in the subway. The eye, they concluded, would be best on the point of the first finger. You could poke it round a corner to see who was coming. You could see straight up or look straight behind. You could put it in your pocket and count your money.

'But the eyes on the front of the face!' said Mack with a shudder of fear in his voice.

I have thought of him every time since that I have caught a pike. It is the mark of the predator. The rabbit has eyes on the sides of the head. The fox has them in front. The partridge has eyes at the sides, allowing him almost all-round vision. The falcon has them in front, giving a binocular overlap for taking aim at speed. Of all the fish we catch in English water only the pike has eyes on the front of the head.

The pike is a villain and therefore a source of excitement to small boys who go fishing. He is a begetter of legends. For centuries past there have been tales of terrible pike. Pike that have fought with swans. Pike that have taken the arms of women who went down to the bank to do the washing. Great pike that have fought duels until they both died, with the head of one locked in the three hundred backward sloping teeth of the other.

Just as I write a journalist has rung to consult me about a monster that has become locally infamous. Thirty pounds they say he weighs, and he has invaded a newly created Leisure Lake where he is eating his own weight of trout every two days. 'We're going to have some fun with him', says the reporter. 'They are calling him Scarface'.

I think that in a comparatively new lake they more likely have two or three pounders. It takes a long time for a pike to grow to thirty pounds, however good the diet. In any case, they'll have to call it 'Mrs Scarface'. All pike of great weight are female. They go to the spawning bed accompanied by two or three much smaller husbands, and often finish the event by eating them. There's women's lib for you!

The pike is admirably designed for its role of the wolf of the stream. The main fins are large and gathered in a group at the tail end. One thrash of the long parallel body delivers the strength of all its muscles to that point – a sudden great thrust of power. It's like a boat with an outsize propeller to which maximum revs can be delivered by ramming down the throttle. The fish is a short-burst hunter – like the cheetah.

The body is camouflaged with greenish vertical stripes and, lying motionless against a bank of reeds, it is very hard to see. In that position the pike itself cannot see much because the binocular vision is restricted to a narrowish angle along the nose.

But as he lies there he is conscious, as a man would be of steady background noise, of the stillness of the lake around him or in a stream of the steady rhythm of the flow. These conditions are monitored for him by his 'live sides', the line of nerve-endings lying along his flank like a keyboard that responds to the tiniest variation of pressure. The swimming of a nearby waterbeetle. The plop of a distant diving water rat. The reverberation from the clay bank of a clumsy man's footstep. And no doubt quite sub-consciously, from the difference of signal strength and the time of arrival at different points he learns accurately about distance, speed and direction. Better indeed than a man who has but two eyes or two ears with which to take cross-bearings. The pike has at least twenty sensors spaced the length of his flank.

When he is curious he will drift towards a signal, swinging the angle of his body to check the direction. When he is interested I suppose he must set his direction so that the impulses are felt equally down both his sides, Then he can forge forward with confidence until his binocular eyes can do the range-finding.

I am sure that the pike usually approaches his prey on sonar control and then switches to visual for the final dash. Long ago when I first went punt-fishing with Uncle Stanley we used to moor at the head of a swim that was favoured by a shoal of dace. After dropping the mudweights to fix the craft in position (two fifty-six pound weights that once belonged to sack-scales) we allowed an interval for peace to descend and then began to feed the swim with ground-bait. Fifteen minutes were usually enough to bring the shoal on the feed and, trotting our floats down the current, we began to catch fish. Eight or ten dace we usually had in the next twenty minutes. Then suddenly all would go quiet. Uncle would say, 'There's a pike moved into the swim'.

After this had happened several times Uncle said – as the mudweights dropped – 'If Jack comes up again today we'll have him', and he fixed up his stronger rod with a big cork float and a tackle of two big triple hooks, and laid it on the floor of the punt.

After we'd had six dace and dropped them in the wet well of the punt he took the sixth and nicked the two triple hooks into its lip and its back fin and then ran it down stream. When he put the rod down the cork float was bobbing just about where we'd taken the dace, and we set off to fish down either side of it. We took another dace, and nothing much else happened; then the pike-rod gave a kick that nearly took it into the water.

Uncle caught it with his left hand and, for a while, did nothing but let the line run out with the old Nottingham Reel clicking. Then he wound up till the line tightened and gave a long heave. The rod shuddered. 'Jack's on' he said, and handed the rod to me.

'Now, take it easy' he said, as I began to feel the power on the other end. 'The current's helping you tire him. Lift the rod, then wind down. Pump him. That's right, pump him.' After a while he rolled over on the surface and I almost dropped the rod. At last he began to tire and, through the tears of stress, I saw, as I pulled him in, his crocodile jaw a little open with the teeth showing. His two eyes focussed right on me. 'Uncle' I cried, 'he's looking at me!'

'Ay' he said.

'They dace never looked at me!'

'Nay, well they couldn't, could they? Only with one eye!'

He weighed nine pounds, and after that we caught dace

in peace for several weeks until another pike arrived to take over the territory. We had him too, and I soon began to give short addresses on pike-fishing in the playground at Miss Harrison's.

That is my excuse for putting a portrait of a particular fish in the story of the past which is certainly not an angling book. The pike was a character in the lore of little country boys. He provided them with the combination of excitement and dread on which they thrived and was the subject of hours of excited conversation. Jack was our nickname for him. Little pike are called jack-pike and it is chiefly them that small boys catch – though it has happened otherwise, as I will tell you later.

For a lifetime after that I went pike-fishing, though now I'm old I can't see the point of it. In younger days we went whatever the weather because pike-fishing is best in wintertime. It was part of the Christmas ceremonies. Eating on Xmas Day. Ferreting on Boxing Day. And the day after that competitive pike-fishing in rain, hail or snow, with three sweaters, a dribbling nose and mittens. John Bickerdyke, a Victorian fishing writer who was a great gentleman, said that if the line started to freeze to the rod you should get your manservant to suck the rodrings to keep it free! The toffs had not adopted the trout totem in those days. The roach which, like the snakes, had never been native to Ireland, was introduced there when an English colonel ordered his batman to load a can of them onto the transport for use as livebait in that land where the pike has been known to grow to fifty pounds.

The biggest pike I ever saw caught weighed 37 lbs. The heaviest I ever caught myself weighed twenty-two. The longest was a good yard long and should have weighed more than either of them – but didn't.

It happened in Kent. For a hundred years the Canterbury Anglers had fished a lake there and in the latter years had come to believe there was a 35-pounder in it. Then came the black news that the lake had been sold to developers and filling-in was soon to start. The big machines arrived and the filling-in gradually advanced across the water. As it grew smaller the anglers doggedly fished on. At last, when only a bit of the lake was left, they decided to have one final day – a sort of fishing funeral so to speak – and I went to join them, taking my pike-fishing tackle.

I cast a pike-spoon into a small creek at one end and as it wobbled and throbbed through the water a great shadow slipped out from under the sedges and followed it along until it came close. Then it turned away. Three more times this happened. Each time the great creature was tempted out by the vibration but turned away from the sight of the spoon.

I borrowed a roach from the keep-net of the nearest fisherman and set it up on a live-bait tackle just beyond the furthest point to which he had advanced. After a while I tried the spoon again. Once again it brought the pike forth and she followed in its trail. I lifted the spoon gently out just as she was in good sight of the livebait. She had it in a moment, just changed gear and rammed her foot down.

That pike weighed seventeen pounds and was as thin as an eel. It had been living out time in the dwindling water with a disappearing diet. By its length it was perhaps fifteen years old and I'm sure that two years earlier when the lake was in its prime they did have their thirty-pounder.

The pike-spoon is said to have been invented when a manservant serving picnic tea dropped a teaspoon over the side of the punt. His master noticed how it lurched and wobbled as it fell through the water. He gave orders for the handle of a silver tablespoon to be cut off and the bowl of it to have a treble hook fixed at the broad end and a swivel at the head. Nobody could count how many pike have been caught on spoons since then. It is customary to tie a tassel of red wool over the rear hook. Some say that is the pike's favourite colour, reminding him perhaps of the red fins of a roach. Others say fish are colourblind and it is just that red produces for them the most visible tone. Anyway, it seems to serve to make it visible as soon as possible for the purposes of aiming.

The most remarkable piece of spoon-fishing happened just as I came home on leave and went to stay at Aldermaston, then a country property temporarily occupied by women in uniform. Many of them were spectators to what happened that day and encouraged it in language never before heard to come from female lips.

My friend Bobby St. John Cooper had decided to go perch-fishing, taking with him a tiny spinning-rod with about a five-pound line and a one-inch copper spoon. Several times he cast and spun back along a bank of sedges. Then, as he began to wind, he found he was caught in the lake bottom. He had given it a couple of hard pulls to see if he could free it when the bottom began to move. And it continued to move – on and on towards the far end of the ten-acre water.

It went on and on irresistibly. In no way could such tackle stop what was now on the other end of it. Endlessly the line ran out, revealing halfway a very unreliable-looking knot left no doubt by Bobby's lad who had borrowed the rod earlier. There were about four turns left on the reel when the monster turned round and headed back with Bobby winding wildly to get back in touch. It went on and on and it was a masterpiece of fishing to keep a strain on the fish without getting smashed. And Bobby who had only one good arm did it with the butt tucked into his left armpit and his right hand on the reel.

At last, as the pike tired with the unaccustomed long distance work, it came to the surface and rolled over exposing a side like a bacon-hog to the accompaniment of shrieks from the Women's Auxiliary Territorial Service.

When finally on the bank it proved to weigh 37 pounds – as was shown by the big scales in the village shop, using all the weights and then adding pounds of sugar. As it lay thrashing and snapping its teeth on the bank, Bobby had struck it on the head with a quart bottle of beer. As he did so it disgorged two fresh Crucian Carp which it had recently eaten, one of a pound and a half and the other a pound and three quarters. Had he stayed his hand it would have weighed forty pounds.

Of course, he caught that fish too early. In previous years he had been chronically infected with the pike-fever; but afterwards we could never get him to go. Anything else would be an anti-climax. 'Bobby' I said, 'you should have caught the fish forty years later.'

Yet he was nearly outclassed on his own waters by two little boys. They passed the window of his village house on their way to the lodge gates, carrying a little rod and a jam-jar. Clearly their ambitions were set no higher than minnows.

Yet no more than half-an-hour later there was shouting in the village street, dogs barking and windows being flung open. From the front door we saw the two little boys struggling with something heavy. Each had pushed his belt in at the gills and out of the mouth and like two horses, they were dragging a great pike, while at the same time trying to hold up their trousers.

'Who caught that?' we cried. 'I did' said the smaller of

the two. They had been standing at the end of the lake where the bottom shelves out very flat. The smaller boy was catching tiny roach and pulling them in up the gravel shelf. Suddenly as he had another a great pike rushed after it – and beached himself! The elder little boy was wearing his wellingtons. As the fish lay stranded he jumped in and kicked it ashore.

That fish was also weighed in the shop but it was several packets of sugar lighter than Bobby's. So his reputation was safe. But I'm convinced that older little boy is now Chief Executive of something.

My own biggest fish was a matter of chance and even some embarrassment. I went with a friend to the River Stour where we wanted to fish for pike by wandering with a bait on a free line and searching under the banks in the pools and round the weed-beds – an enjoyable method but needing some skill. I had volunteered to catch the bait for him and soon sent him off with four or five dace in a can. I continued to catch good roach and dace and my keep-net, getting crowded, was at intervals stirred by their struggles. Then suddenly it suffered a great wrench and as I dragged it out most of the bait-fish fell out through a hole in the side.

I cobbled it up with a piece of line and then, fetching a pike-rod from the car, set up a live-bait on what we call a bomb-paternoster that held it in position close to the keep-net. When my friend returned for more bait, having caught a 12 and a 13 pound pike, I was just landing a 22 pounder.

Such a series of tales abut great pike may suggest that the catching of them is quite usual. It is not. The majority of pike-fishing days pass without any fish at all; but the feeding habits of the fish are such that every so often they result in unforgettable bumper days.

As a little jack it lives on the minute water-creatures – water-fleas and shrimps, worms and tadpoles and the fry of other fish. At this stage the boy occasionally catches them on the worms and maggots with which he goes roach-fishing.

But soon the pike turns mostly to fish-food and soon learns to tackle them when they are bigger than he seems likely to manage. He seizes his prey across the middle and, holding it in his crocodile jaws, squeezes it into helplessness. Then, turning it round, he swallows it head first. In this he is aided by his great mass of teeth, spreading in ranks even over the roof of the mouth and the tongue, and all pointing backwards. Any trip down the throat of a pike is a one-way journey. Pike like an occasional water-rat, and a friend of mine made an artificial one with fur and feathers which he used to skitter vainly over the surface. They are devils for ducklings. A pair of tufted on our local lake hatched about a dozen every year but never managed to rear more than one. The pike and the mink had the rest. Again my ingenious friend attached hooks to a celluloid bathroom duck – together with a propeller to produce enticing vibrations. That didn't do any good.

When the pike is well-fed he seems to be uninterested in food. I once watched a big pike lying still in the river while a shoal of roach drifted all around him. Then comes some stimulus, some fascinating set of vibrations he is unable to resist. Sometimes when one pike goes on the rampage he will stimulate the others. The excitement will grow as the tumult in the water increases and you will get one of those pike days.

I once took my little son to the pit behind the Butt Inn at Aldermaston. It was the first day of the Christmas holidays, with frost and brilliant sunshine. We caught forty

pike that day in all sizes. They seized everything that we
threw in the water and two of the smaller fish were grabbed
by bigger ones while we had them on the hook. He thought
he had been introduced to the world's greatest pike-fishery
and went back every day of the holidays – but never saw
another fish!

Despite the fact that most methods of pike-fishing – from
Walton working a troll-bait with a pumping action to the
tremor of the spoon and the struggling of a live-bait – have
depended on the creation of vibrations, it has more recently
been discovered that the hunting tyrant is quite willing to
pick up dead fish from the lake bottom. Quite often now
you will see the pike-angler buying himself a dozen herrings.
Perhaps it is a civic duty? Perhaps he has the job of scaveng-
ing the environment. It would be a job because there are
no vibrations to help him here. He would have to quarter
the lake low down and use his eyes. Two weeks ago, when
some trout were being put in a local water, six of them
died en route. They lay on the surface and drifted over to
the downwind shore. There they fell to the bottom and
were visible in a row in three feet of water. They were
gone in the morning.

Which makes you think about eating pike as people used
to do. You can forget it! They are inedible. The French will
swallow them but only in the company of one of their
famous sauces.

Only one modern author has claimed that they are delicious – Brian Vesey-Fitzgerald – but let me tell you that
his recipe for making them so required the addition of the
following – beef suet and grated bread, nutmeg, shredded
lemon peel, three hard-boiled eggs, a pint of shrimps in
beef gravy, stewed mushrooms, a quart of oysters, a tumbler
of port and a pound of butter.

9
The Fellows who cut the Hay

It is said by some clever people that English country-folk are so wary of personal communication that they bring up the subject of weather on first meeting in order to fend off more intimate matters – a smart crack that could come only from someone who gets his living indoors.

For centuries we have known that a day of rain or a fortnight without it can affect a whole season's prosperity, and that in our island climate neither can be reliably predicted. Despite millions of pounds of technology country people get little comfort from weathermen whose most positive suggestion is 'I think I should take an umbrella' – an exclusively urban implement. I sometimes recall with trepidation that Eisenhower sent three hundred and fifty thousand men to the beaches on the advice of a meteorologist.

Still, the great gale of October 1987 gave them a warning to get off the 'game shows' and attend to their work. Nowadays they can't wait to tell us about the wind. Previously they hardly seemed to mention it.

Country people remember the years of their lives by the weather. I, for instance, can bring to life 1921 and 1922 exactly on account of what happened in hay time. Every year in those days the prosperity of small holdings depended on what happened to the hay. Mother used to say the Old Man wasn't fit to talk to in hay time.

Yet the absence of hay making is one of the things that would astound the Old Man if he were to drive through today's landscape. Not a lot is made now, and that chiefly for consumption by 'saddle horses'. It is worth recalling what a slice of life it used to be.

Even the name of the stuff is interesting. Originally 'hay' did not mean grass, it meant a 'hedge'. Most of the cleared land was in big open fields. Over them and across the waste the animals grazed freely. Certain small fields were enclosed to keep them out and it is surprising how many field names on today's farms derive from that. On our place we had Picket Close and Ram's Close.

To make a close you dug a ditch and threw up a bank on top of which you planted a hedge – a 'hay'. Villages in England like Layer-de-la-Haye, and in Normandy like La Haye du Puits, meant places that had been fenced in. If you know a man called Mr Hayward he is descended from the fellow who used to look after the hedges.

So the grass that grew protected so it might be cut for the winter was called haygrass. Grandfather always called it that. He used to say, 'We've led the haygrass'. The Old Man said, 'We've carried the hay.' So the language moved on a bit between them, even though one had learned the art from the other. And art it was. Even Fream's *Elements of Agriculture* – the old bible of the craft – was reduced to saying that it depended chiefly on experience and hereditary skill.

It is the art of juggling with moisture. If you can put a crop of grass in store at 15% humidity it will keep its nourishment right through the winter. If it is put away just two or three per cent too moist it will rot, and sometimes set fire to itself by spontaneous combustion. If it is just a bit too dry it will crumble into a fibrous mass of no worthwhile feed value.

First you have to decide when to cut it. It is fullest of

nourishment when the grasses and clovers and vetches are just in bloom. Before that there will not be enough weight in the crop. A little later the seed has formed and will be knocked out by the hay-making and left for the birds, and the stems will begin to dry out hard and white. The Old Man would be out among it two or three times a day looking for the point of perfection. After supper he would be outside staring at the sky and trying to decide whether to cut in the morning.

Cutting started at day break because all other haymaking tasks had to wait for the dew to dry off so, if the Old Man said 'Cutting in the morning' we knew we would have to be up to milk in the dark.

I can remember the time when the hay was cut with scythes – just the tail end of it. The horse machine-mower came in just about when I was born but took a long time to spread all over. When you first saw scythe-mowers at work you thought the yonger men were working much harder than the old. They were, but they were not cutting faster. In fact, the old men got down the row first because it was a matter of balance and angle and height. Grandfather was one of the best. You could hear the difference without looking. His was a long even rasping noise as the stroke cut all the way and made the others sound like chop-chop-chop. He would cut level at a chosen height – no point in picking up dry stalk-bottoms – and alter the handles on his sned to fix the amount of stubble.

There was no use for boys at scythe mowing but with the pair-horse mower a lad was needed on hand all the time. The knife would cut well only for an hour or two and then had to be changed. You had to clamp the knife onto the field gate and get down with the file to both edges of each of its fifty cutters. When the driver shouted 'knife' you had to be ready with a sharp one to carry over to him.

The machine cut a four-foot swathe of grass and by the time the dew was off the swathes would be lying side by side across the field, committed to fate. The word, of course, is one that has gone into the language but is now often used with its pronunciation degraded. You do not cut a 'swaythe' through something: you cut a 'sworthe'.

The rest of the haymaking was carried out with four one-horse vehicles known as the swathe-turner, siderake, tedder and horse-rake – subtly employed in differing order and sequence. It is, perhaps, best to imagine them at work on one of the very few occasions when hay-making went perfectly. At the same time this will remind us how it was done without benefit of machine – in the dimly remembered days of hayforks and sunbonnets. Indeed, while the hay-harvest was in progress on the farm, little patches of cot-tagers' hay could be seen being made on the roadsides, the commons and under the apple trees.

The swathes that were cut at dawn were left just long enough for the dew to dry off and then they had to be fluffed up so that the sun and the breezes could get into the row. The tedder, which was like four combs on a revolv-ing axle, would tease up a small row nicely if you set it to turn backwards. Turning forwards, in line with the prog-ress of the machine, it would scatter the grass high in the air to land in a long, loose heap. In earlier days the tedding was done by rows of old men, women and children work-ing along with hay forks – light tined forks with shoulder-high handles of the sort that are still seen in stable-yards where they are often now called pitchforks. A pitchfork is another matter, as will be seen later.

It has been known for hay to be made in a day, when the crop was light and the sun intensely hot, but usually it all has to be rolled up again just before the next dew falls in the evening. The side-rake does this, rolling the fluffy band up into a single sausage. Only the outside of this will receive the dew, with the sun-blessed hay inside remaining dry. This, again, was once done by hand, with wooden hayrakes two to a row, usually with the haymakers working fast and quiet to beat the evening – unlike the songs and chatter of the tedding time.

Next day it all starts again and the hay is once more tedded to spend a half day in the breeze. With luck by early afternoon the Old Man may declare it ready to carry and the side-rake rolls it up again. A simple task really – once in twenty years!

In contrast to such ideal times is the infinite number of changes and shifts that must be undertaken to beat the English weather. Turning the rows over with the swathe-turner rather than risk loosening them out. Carting on through the dew of the evening rather than risk rain that promised before morning. Cutting on a rainy morning on the gamble that it will stop before the hay begins to wilt. Keeping the work going on several different cuts that are taking the weather at different stages, with the boys trotting the cobs across the fields to tedd out one piece and then roll up another. In the last resort putting it up in cocks. Each drop of rain leaches goodness out of the stuff and its quality drops. Finally, when there is just a little value left and the rain still comes, it is piled up in conical heaps with the tops smoothed to shed the continuing rain in the hope of saving something. 'Well', I've heard the Old Man say more than once. 'We'll put it in cocks and go to the pictures.' He was a specialist in taking things on the chin and not moaning. It was a sad phrase to hear. There weren't many farmers at market while the June sun shone. Then one day there would be quite a few turning up. 'How's the hay, then?' 'We cocked it up.' It meant we have failed and are praying that we may save something of it.

Once each cut was dry – and its quality would be good or bad according to how we had nipped the work in between the weather – it was time to carry. In my childhood I worked through the whole history of how this was done.

At first the waggon was led between two rows by a boy, with the loader on board. Two men each walked his row and worked with a giant pitchfork, twice his own height with sprung eighteen inch tines and a springy ash handle twelve feet long. The fork was pushed along the row to build up a hay-cock five foot high, then the loader turned the handle over and leaped in the air for his weight to drive the points in. You could hear the crunch. Then he turned round, put his shoulder half-way along the handle and levered the whole lot into the air. He held it there balanced, with one hand at his waist and the other stretched high above, and staggered to put it up just where the loader called for it. The weight and pressure must be spread evenly over the waggon if a big load were to travel without tumbling.

When the last pitch was up the boy would unhook the great hayrope and pitch it over from side to side – from cleat to cleat – and, when the loader had settled it in, tie on. Then at a shout from above the men would throw their pitchforks in a wide arc to land on their points far enough away to be seen from the top. Once they were wobbling there·the man on top would slide right down the back of the load. You could tell a loader by the shine on his pants and his wide leather leg-yokes done up tight to stop his trousers running up.

Then came the lad's responsibility. It was not too much

to lead the waggon across one field to a rick building the other side; but, if the work was going on half-a-mile away at the rickyard, it was another matter. An extra horse would be taken off the hedge and chained on the front; then, with the curve up to the gate, the turn into the track and the bends and slopes from then on, it was heart in the mouth all the way. And some way along you'd meet another boy with an empty waggon. If you didn't meet him then it meant they'd stopped work at the yard. It was Bavertime.

We had two outdoor meals on a haymaking day, never sat on a chair after breakfast. The first was called Baver and the second Tea. 'Baver' comes from 'bouvoir' the Norman-French for 'to drink'. The hinged front of a helmet that can be raised is called the Beaver – for the same reason. Mother used to pack splendid food in an apple-basket covered with a white cloth – including her famous pasties that she made in dozens at hay-time. The casual workers brought whatever they had for Baver. Old Jim Hynes was the man to watch.

When we'd put the nosebags round the horses Jim would take out his lambfoot knife and wipe in on his trousers. Then he would cover thick slices of bread with a cold bacon rasher, to be covered in turn with a deep layer of rings cut from a big, raw onion. On top again went a piece of cheese, cut to fit. The result was at least two inches thick and he would shove the corner in his mouth and anchor it there with his two or three remaining teeth. To make further progress it was necessary to cut the whole thing off at the lips with the lambfoot. He was always happy at haytime. The brewery at Rowsham used to drop a niner in the hedge every two days. Nobody showed any signs of it – they lost too much in perspiration.

We kept up loading with pitchforks until Jim Hynes

died. He died at work, quite suddenly and shockingly. A visitor from town was giving a hand, clearing up the rows behind the pitchers with a small hayfork. When the load was topped up and the pitchers tossed their forks out to stand in view, he leaned his against the back of the load – just where Jim came sliding down on his backside. He would never have believed that any of us in the field, from our disciplined childhood onward, had not learned to do things properly.

After he went we got a hay-loader. He always said he would never work with one because it pitched all the hay up at the back of the waggon and he couldn't call his shots to build properly. It was a tall, roller conveyor that was driven by its own wheels and picked up a whole row neatly. When the load was up the lad could back up the thill-horse an inch and lift the thing off its tow-bar.

At this time there also came hay-sweeps – great flat wooden forks with iron shod points. They lay flat on the ground like an egg fork and were dragged by one horse each side (later pushed from behind by a tractor). They were no good to us because we snapped the tines. On smoother ground they went right across the field, gathering a mountain and delivering it at the rick.

In this fever of mechanisation we also bought a rick-elevator to go with the hay-loader. It was like an escalator and could be wound up to deliver higher and higher as the rick grew.

It was driven by an old horse walking round in a circle, one who'd done his time pulling heavy loads. He quite liked the job except that he kept falling asleep. The boy who was clearing round the rick and picking up the pieces and had to spring into action when the whole thing stopped. 'What are you doing down there? Wake the horse up!'

The ricks went up like the loads, though much higher with the weight carefully spread so that as they sank they sank square, and the ridge clean and sharp to shed moisture. We rarely got up there in a day so – with the slightest chance of rain – the huge, heavy rick-sheet had to be pulled up on a sort of rugger goal-post frame and then hung round the edges with old iron from the barn. That was it for the day, except that the cows were now bursting to be milked in the dark.

In the end it would all be over with just time to sit down before harvest time, after which Old Jim would come down with straw to thatch the settled ridges against the winter. With one of them he would usually win the district thatching prize, together with the hedge-laying, to say nothing of being placed in the hurdle-making which he also thought he should have won each year.

There would be ricks in each of the fields all waiting for the hay-dealer. When he came to buy he would bring a long iron rod, barbed at the end like a fish hook. He would push it right into the middle of the rick and then pull it out by its ring to get a sample from the middle and sniff it. Good hay smells beautiful and bad hay has no smell, but poor hay that has been heated up can sometimes produce a scent that will fool some of the people. The Old Man wasn't beyond trying it on. He too had a hay-rod and I've known him push it into a rick in which he'd risked a bit of moisture, then spit on its end to see if it was hot. Once he took it too far. We had to pull a whole rick down and spread it to avoid a fire.

In the yard there would be an army of ricks behind the byre. They would feed the animals through the winter. We had to cut the air out in tall square columns with a hay-knife. Don't speak of it! You see them hanging on the walls of pubs. People say 'That's a hayknife. I remember them.' If they did I think they would turn silently away. Working in a settled rick with a hayknife – particularly up a ladder – would make a good punishment for a penal camp.

It has stirred me to remember it, and I know a lot of older people will read it with emotion. Anyway, it is a good thing to record how to do it lest oil gives out and we find we have forgotten. It's quite possible. I am quite sure for instance, that we in England forgot for some centuries how to make silage. There was none about when I was young. Yet James Fisher told me that when he and Peter Scott went to the interior of Iceland to ring the Pinkfoot Geese, they found many stone silage pits that had been used a thousand years ago in that land so unsuitable for hay-making. You'd think it must have come over to us with the Vikings.

However, we discovered in the war that a rackety, smelly and sometimes poisonous system had taken the place of hay-making. It works not by controlling moisture but by exactly controlling putrefaction. It can be made independent of the weather. But you couldn't make it in quantity without diesel.

I thought that I should never see the old summertime sights again. However, as I drove across Germany in 1945, when the Wehrmacht were cooped up in Schleswig-Holstein, there were the German women and children, sunbonnets and all, trying to make hay with forks and wooden rakes. But Montgomery had an idea of what was needed. The first thing he did was to organise a great convoy – called Exercise Barleycorn – to bring the German country lads out from behind the barbed-wire and take them back to their villages.

10

Dramatis Personae

There is a dialect of rural English that is used more widely than any other yet is never spoken by country people. It is heard all the way from the Two Ronnies to Midsummer Night's Dream and is spoken exclusively on the Archers. It is called Mummerset.

Shakespeare, I'm sure, spoke the Warwickshire tongue but when he came down to London and the Court he met those who used the south-eastern dialect that subsequently forked into Standard English on one side and Cockney on the other. Such people, at the centre of wealth and power, would have already built up their idea of themselves and come to need some way of expressing their attitudes to the yokels. So I am sure that at the Globe Theatre, Shakespeare's Bottom was already played in Mummerset. 'Oh-aagh!' It has been put to very wide use.

The real local dialects, on the other hand, were very confined in their circulation, belonging to mini-cultures extending just as far as a good road-pony could travel in a day. As late as the early Thirties the British Drama League sent a recording team round England to talk to native people. In more than a hundred places they recorded a set piece, a sample of local impromptu talk and an attempt at a passage of Shakespeare. It was quite astounding; in some places they gathered two or three quite different modes of speech within a single county. You could never get them again. We never heard Southern English spoken in our house – except now and again when hounds were drawing near and hunting folk came to breakfast – until 2LO started broadcasting the Nine o'Clock News. After that we were never the same again.

The old people, of course, were unchangeable and kept their speech. A visitor from London got up early in the morning and met Jim Hynes. 'Lovely Day', he said, and received the astonishing reply, 'Attle reyan. Them mollyons be aggled' – which is to be translated 'It will rain. The herons are excited.' In the West Country the elderly continued to omit prepositions, and articles – 'I be just going farm'. In the North Uncle Joe continued to upbraid rumbustious children with 'Stop laikin about like a cock baht yed!' Mother still called a sofa a langsaddle and a clothes-airer a winteredge. Even if they lost some of the language they kept their turn of mind. On the night after we watched the lunar landings Old Mrs. White next door went out to the privy and saw the moon above. She ran back in the house and said to her son, 'That moon's still up there. I thought them fellers wennen gottit.'

It was typical of the tiny communities where the little languages grew that Old Jim, at the age of seventy, was still considered a foreigner. He had come from just over the county boundary at the age of seventeen but something in his voice told on him. It was probably in the vowels.

Those vowels! It makes me sad that I was filled with so much Latin and Greek and never taught the early English and the Anglo-Saxon. I believe there are philological rules to explain how as the tongues changed in some places the letter A turned from Ah to Oh when it had a W in front – 'warm', 'walk', 'water'. In the North we still said 'Wahm' and 'Watter'. And an explanation of why the vowels opened up as you travelled from east to west. The name for a female sheep went – yew, yo, yow. A trough changed

from troff to tro to trow. The wooden hammer that drove
in the fencing stakes changed from beetle to bittle and
beyetle. Differences of spelling hint at some of the things
that make English seem so odd to foreigners. I used to
think it was a genteel mannerism to pronounce White and
While as if the H were in front of the W. But in Anglo-Saxon
days the H was in front of the W – Hwite and Hwile.

None of it can be reproduced in writing. I defy anyone
to write down how Horace White, who was our cowman,
said the word 'cow'. When a tail flapped in his ear, or a
shuffling foot splashed the bucket, he would growl, 'Starnd
still stupid cayew! Ent yer got no knowledge?' And that
is another failure.

The man who tried hardest to reproduce one of these
modes of speech and, for my money, failed – was William
Barnes, the Dorset poet. I knew an old fellow who had all
his poems by heart and, when he spoke them, they had a
native reality. But the jumble of letters that Barnes used
for the printed versions is meaningless. There can never
have been such a language, I think. He must have invented
the whole thing.

But when I sit in the pub with Archie, observing the
younger generation, he says to me 'Weem both wold'. Tom
and Alfie, sitting in the old bar, give me a daily picture of
the local past. One tall, big-boned and a bit reddish, the
other small, neat and dark. The Saxon who came up the
river with his axe, and the Briton who came down from
the chalk.

Nowadays the young people speak more and more
widely with the voice of David Frost, a back-cross between
the genteel and vulgar versions of the south-eastern dialect,
developed in the laboratory of liberated higher education.
But not so long ago even those who held power in the

districts spoke the local tongue. Most of the squires were yokels. Old Sir Roger de Coverley was certainly a figure of fun when he went to London. Raleigh was at home in the inn at Henstridge on his way home to Sherborne; at least he was until the potman threw a jug of cold water over him when the smoke rose for the first time publicly from his pipe.

Directly to the south of him as he sat there lay the Vale of the Little Dairies which is sprinkled still with little manor-houses, hardly bigger than the larger farm-houses and differing from them hardly at all except for a porch that carries a coat of arms. Some of them are thatched. To one side of each lies an old garden, to the other a farmyard.

The small squires who built these houses were the bottom layer of the nobility. They came into existence through the need of the Crown for fighting-men. One of the medieval monarchs is known to have created nearly a thousand of them at one time. In exchange for maintaining a horse and armour and responding without hesitation to the King's call to service, leading with them the 'jackmen', the leather-jacketed local conscripts, they were granted knighthood and some feudal privileges that put them above common people. Some of them had considerable estates and some with nearly nothing were as seedy as Don Quixote, seeking their living as mercenaries in between calls from the Crown.

They lived under the shadow of the grandees who owned great sweeps of the country. They married their youngest daughters, embellishing their own coats of arm with emblems from those of their wives' families. In pursuit of distinction they also joined their names together, produc-ing in hundreds the famous double-barrelled appellations to which the English have always accorded respect.

They mostly got their living from the land and, under the authority of the Lord Lieutenant, they held the small offices of power. As a child I knew Garratt-Pegge as the name of the local JP, and Selby-Lowndes as the Master of Foxhounds. They had their portraits painted – a thing that seems to set them apart – and hung them alongside their ancestors. They sat in the squire's pew in the days when the church music was played by little woodwind and string bands.

This was before the days when technology forced us into centralised authority and in terms of local people the Squire held real power. It was he who decided who would have a farm, where the footpaths ran, whether the village could have a reading-room. And there were good and bad of him – as with policemen, parsons and doctors. Under a good squire a man knew he had a protector. A widow knew she would keep her cottage all her days, with her welfare looked out for. As for the bad? I knew one who rode his estate on an Arab pony, shouting abuse and orders like a regimental sergeant-major. One day he said to a shepherd, 'Where's your son? He finished school and he hasn't come to the estate yard.'

'Ah well, Squire' said the man, 'begging your pardon. He's got himself employment.'

'How can he have? He hasn't even seen the agent!'

'Well, Sir, he had the building trade in mind. He's got himself taken on. Pony boy, carting stuff and making the tea and such.'

'Well, he can forget that! Tell him to see the Agent in the morning! Or get out of your cottage by Friday!'

Rich or poor – and some of the squires were often in patched trousers during the long periods of agricultural depression – they were accorded great respect. The first time I motored through the southern English countryside we came into a village where the headlights revealed three old men leaning on their sticks in the dark and the rain. In unison they raised their right hands to their foreheads. They didn't know who we were but took it for granted that a motor-car must contain their betters.

'Good God!' I thought, coming from the hard northern land of the Moss Troopers to whom even the Roman legions had given a wide berth.

It was a culture that took little account of class but set great store by 'station'. Wherever they would go later, the squires' children started their education with everyone else at the village school. Cottage lads wrestled in the playground with other little boys who would one day have the power to set them up in farmsteads. Little ladies flocked up for protection with other girls who would one day be parlour-maids. Miss Harrison once caught me and young Tyrwhitt-Drake up a tree and led us off each by one ear.

It was a complicated culture and could only have worked because it was accepted at all levels. I sometimes think that the importance of fox-hunting in the countryside was that it provided a symbolic expression of the relationships. With the excitement shared by all, from the Master to the hedge-cutter, with costume ritualised according to station, with Christian names used across the boundaries – including for Charlie, the totem animal whose habits were under-stood by all. Everyone was in some kind of relationship with everyone else.

On a narrower level the Yeomanry also epitomised the relationship. Again, Christian names passed between the young squires and richer yeoman farmers who rode their hunters in officer's uniform and the men of the countryside who served on their cobs as troopers.

But it has to be remembered that when, at the time of Speenhamland, the farm-workers marched for higher wages, it was the son of a local squire who led the Dragoons against them. Protest in those earlier days was branded as riot, and the arms that had been borne four or five centuries still carried the feudal duty of preserving the King's Peace.

Still most of the time the whole thing hung together and the squires, in their comparatively modest manor-houses, belonged to the countryside on which they depended for their means.

There was a wide gap between them and the Big House people. These grandees, in whose shadow most of the country squires lived, came from the bigger world of Windsor and Westminster. Their huge fortunes came from banking and trade monopolies, from mining rights, the prizes of war and the loot of empire. Their sons rode with the Household Cavalry and their daughters spoke the jargon of the Court – though some of them were fluent in Mummerset when telling comical stories about the yokels. To them those whom the squires regarded fraternally were a mob.

In grandfather's youth the Big House people were in a state of nerves about the mob. They had bad dreams about them and were haunted by a dread that the French Revolution would spread worldwide. All the discontents of small country people that arose from the international changes of trade were interpreted as evidence of the creeping threat of Jacobinism. At the time on many of their estates, they added to their follies and gazebos tall look-outs and belvederes, set on the highest point where a beacon could be lit to carry a signal to one of the places where detachments of militia – the 'landowners private army' – were kept in readiness.

Yet when the real threat arose from Jacobinism it was, largely, the yokels who stood against it, officered by their local country gentlemen. The Wiltshires marched against Napoleon singing a coarse market song of their own district:-
> And when she got to Salisbury
> Her butter and eggs were sold.
> And there she had a tale to tell
> That will make your blood run cold.
> She said 'I lost my maidenhead
> To a man that I adore.
> Now he's a rollicking sailor boy,
> And I'm a bloody whore.'

It's surprising how often the owners of the Great Houses changed, unlike the squires whose names are to be seen in the local churchyard over five hundred years. The time came quite early when the grant of land was the foundation of fortune. Privateering, merchant adventuring, monopolies, the politics of the Court, the spread of the Empire, slavery, sugar, banking, iron – all these changed and stirred up their fortunes. In the end we had Leeds seated in Kent, Norfolk in Sussex and Devonshire in Derbyshire. Somersets in Wiltshire. Sugar barons in Dorset. Yorkshire coal-owners in Hampshire. Moneylenders in Bucks.

They came intermittently to their great estabishments – nowadays often in the hands of the National Trust and used as television locations. In my infancy they came in convoys of wooden-wheeled Rolls Royces, giant Napiers and Isotta-Fraschinies embellished with silver lamps and curling horns, all designed to give comfort for the passengers while the chauffeur sat outside in the rain. Grandfather had seen them arrive in their road coaches, with livered grooms riding ahead to clear away flocks of sheep and market carts and a waggonette full of lackeys following behind. There are still a few such coaches hidden away in the coach-houses under dustsheets, almost as grand as those in the Royal Mews. They were in the business of grandeur.

Apart from such comings and goings we rarely saw them and, in fact, knew little about them; apart from the many myths and folk-tales that originated from those servants that were drawn from the district. The army of gardeners managing a landscape and producing figs and grapes under glass. The squadron of gamekeepers, and the shooting-coachman who drove the brakes and never went to London with the family. The stable-boys and laundry-women and house-maids. In all their gossip the owner of the big house was referred to as 'Lordy' and the tales that were told of him stretched your eyes. The many bright girls who went up there to be house-maids learned arts and manners that enabled them later to enhance the style of a farmer's household. Now and again one of them would return rather early, and in a state that was referred to as 'weighing a bit heavier'. Not many tears were shed over that. She was poor and she was honest, but she knew when she was onto a good thing.

In our district we had a farmer, on a very good holding, who was the spitting image of 'Lordy!' If you'd seen them both in bathing trunks you couldn't have told them apart. His mother had gone up as a housemaid.

The tale is told of a senior American Officer who during the war was entertained at one of the Great Houses. 'Tell me, Sir' he asked the owner, 'how do you manage to maintain such a splendid staff of servants?'

'We breed 'em', Lordy replied.

11

Time and the Moving Men

Each week I set my watch by the digital time-signal that appears in the corner of the television when you press the right button. That signal comes from a clock which – a retired Telecom engineer tells me – is really three clocks, each as big as a house, each governed by the inevitable pulse of a vibrating crystal, each made from twenty metals so that their expansions hold each other in check, and each keeping a watching eye on the others. I find that my watch – which is a modest one by today's standards – never varies by more than three seconds a week. Two and a half minutes a year!

I doubt if Grandfather's gold hunter which I still have, and which is a masterpeice of craftsmanship, was ever within two and a half minutes of the right time. Not the watch's fault. He had no sure way of setting it right.

Of course, the church clock was several centuries old but, for most of its life, it had to be set from a sundial. I once decided to put a post in the kitchen garden that would tell me when the pub opened on Sunday. You have to get the post perfectly vertical with a spirit-level and then put a peg in the ground at the very end of its shadow. As the shadow moves you put more pegs in and as the morning progresses they will grow gradually nearer the post.

You seek the line along which the shadow lies shortest because the sun is highest. Allowing for the fact that you cannot measure shadows precisely because they have fuzzy ends, you are now at just about 12 noon. Opening time on Sunday. Except for the fact that the sun never shines when you want to consult it and, anyway, the sun doesn't know about Summer Time.

I suppose that accurate time first came to the country when the stage-coaches and post-chaises travelled the new improved roads. The coach guard with his big turnip watch. The rich couple posting across the land with a change of horse every dozen miles; the lady holding on her lap one of the clever little coach-clocks, safe in its leather case. Nowhere would either of them be more than half a week from the bells of Westminster.

Then, during great-grandfather's manhood, came the steam train, installing across the land the great system of railway clocks – all within a day of the terminals. From them the time could be carried by the people who moved into the deep countryside. Even the church clocks began to strike approximately on time. Even so, people who had always lived by 'cockscrow' or sunset were suspicious of it. 'What time have you got?' they would say – rather than 'What time is it?'

The church bells were beyond our hearing and time came to us either with Mark Howe the cattle-dealer against whose ample belly an impressive watch was snuggled; or with Tommy Ricketts, the higgler, who had picked up some sort of watch in one of his deals. It was always shaken hard and held to the ear before being consulted.

Of the two I preferred Tommy. The dealer seemed to me a threatening man. He had a loud voice and his laughter appeared to be aroused mainly by tales of other people's misfortunes. He had money and liked to exercise power over those in need of it. He had an eerie knowledge of everyone's cattle. Once, as he passed our herd, he waved his stick at one of them and said, 'I sold you her as a rearing calf. Six years come February.'

The higgler spoke in a quiet voice, even when alone
with you as if not to be overheard, and gave the impression
that what he said was for no other ears. Yet he was liked
by everyone for miles. Mother always sat him down to a
good tea. He had a knack of getting her talking. He must
have known the inside story of every family in the district.

The higgler was really a wandering car-boot sale. Where-
ever he went he picked up what wasn't wanted and found
a home for it somewhere down the line. He could get you
almost anything insignificant. Ask him for a few yards of
pig-wire and you'd get it – usually three months after the
pig was killed. He never seemed to handle much money
but did it all by 'chopping'. He would exchange half a roll
of binder twine for a fagging hook. He would 'chop' you
a sitting of eggs for a couple of rabbit-traps. As he came
slowly down the track on his crazily loaded trolley, behind
his beloved old horse, we would rush to the gate to see
what he had on board. He had that old horse from us. We
chopped it for a sacklift and two milking pails.

Sometimes, if he came to us on a Saturday, I would ride
on with him and sleep in the stable of one of the far farms
while he pegged his horse out and dossed under the trolley.
In the morning the lady would give me a sandwich to put
in my right-hand pocket – the left already had a catapult
and some rabbit-wires – and I would take the whole day
to walk back. No sense in arriving in time for evening
chapel.

I was sure that I wanted to grow up to be a higgler.
Higglers, I could see, never did a day's work and never
stayed two days in the same place. There came a time in
the lives of small country boys – living in a fifteen mile
circle of which they knew every yard – when they got

fascinated by the moving people; the ones who came in from somewhere else and disappeared goodness knows where, connecting up the scores of small private worlds.

The Rabbit Skin lady came only once a year and, if you hadn't know how nice she was, you'd have sworn she was a witch. She would come leading her donkey cart down a village street with the children all dancing. On her head was a straw-boater painted with tar to keep the rain out – just like Nelson's sailors. She swore at the donkey through her three remaining teeth. Her nailed boots struck sparks and she shoved her hand in her apron pocket to pelt the kids with liquorice allsorts.

Her stock-in-trade was just liquorice allsorts and jam-jars. The cart was full of jam-jars and she would chop them for only one thing – rabbit skins. The product of a year's rabbiting, legitimate or otherwise, was bundled up in the sheds awaiting her arrival. The cottage women boiled the jars pretty thoroughly before using them for damsons and plums and jam, since it was believed that she collected them from the dustbins in more populous places and washed them just a little in the streams along the way. The donkey knew just where to stop while she called for a pint. His memory for country pubs was remarkable for her territory must have been enormous and somewhere in the middle of it was a hat-factory awaiting the product of her travels.

There was no obvious rhythm in the wanderings of the Umbrella Man. He was a tiny man of unsavoury appearance and he just turned up intermittently, perhaps when he was not confined elsewhere or more likely when he was being sought elsewhere and had to keep away from the workhouses and the turnpike roads.

He certainly didn't come for the trade. Apart from the Vicar and certain farmers' wives with pretentions, nobody had an umbrella to mend. And nobody was going to buy an umbrella when there was a good corn-sack handy of which the corner could be turned in to make a hood. But he usually had several for sale which may have been hopeless cases that he had been given and had managed to cobble up; or perhaps they had just been snatched from a church porch some miles away.

He was a remarkable performer on the tin piccolo and played to himself as he shuffled along, draped with all his stuff, trilling little tunes that made you feel that there must be some good in him. He also played outside the door of the inn in the evening until someone called him to play a request. Under his influence the evening would take a musical turn, with his whistle providing the background to such fine old songs as 'My old swan went whim-wham' and 'Where be that blackbird, George?' Finally, the singers would be bellowing unaware that they had no accompaniment and he would be sitting in a stupor with his whistle to his lips. He would be gone in the morning.

Although I was born too late to know them I often heard talk of the wandering weavers. Quite a few of the farms still had handlooms in the loft and there were spinning-wheels all around. We still had three pairs of heavy linen sheets woven from flax grown on the farm and spun by great-grandma. Woollen yarn also would be spun and the clatter of the loom could be heard through the house when the travelling weaver was making his stay.

The men never liked the weaver. He was too long alone with the women. He knew all that was going on and, sitting up in the attic window, he had a good idea when the men were working far from home. Those were days of large families and all children were treated with equal justice but now and again a husband would look at one of them and wonder if he didn't have a look of the weaver about him.

In the days before modern transport the shepherds too were moving men. Every year they walked their flocks along the tracks and droves to the great sheep fairs, Down to Wilton next to Salisbury – capital of the southern country – the tracks come out of the chalk like the legs of a spider. These were the sheep highways and the flocks came down on them from perhaps a hundred miles around. Against one of those tracks is a farm settlement called Shapwick, and that is the Saxon for sheep farm. In Buckinghamshire they needed the Wiltshire Horn rams to produce the best cross bred mutton and every so often a shepherd would walk all the way to Wilton with his dog to bring back a flock of young rams. In the clay vale below us they discovered early on (I wonder how?) that lambs brought up from the Romney Marsh would fatten at record speed on their early spring grass. Every year a farmer would drive his pony a hundred and fifty miles, taking a shepherd with him, to buy them. When the deal was done he drove back and the shepherd recruited three or four local lads to help him in the great drive. Having arrived with the lambs they usually stayed. When I was a young man the commonest surname in several of the vale villages was Kent.

The sheep lived on the hills and the shepherds often spent long periods high up in their huts without returning to the cottages in the valley below. Many of them filled their solitude playing the pipe. The dogs lay beside them and the sheep were quiet and secure within the sound of music. Many of the oldest folk tunes were born from this. In the intervals of the music shepherds could often be heard talking to themselves and many of them were expert knitters – particularly the ones in the Scottish Highlands.

Once, when I was wandering through the mountains of

Yugoslavia, I made a charming discovery concerning shepherds' pipes. In that country there live the only white Moslems left over from the days of conquest by the Ottoman Empire. You cannot tell to which religion the next valley belongs until you come over the pass and look down to see whether the village has a church or a mosque. According to which you can know if the shepherds' pipes which are still played will be in our own eight-note scale or in another that has the sound of Moorish music. I heard both of them as I crossed the Balkan hills, but didn't see a Balkan shepherd knitting. I did photograph a lady spinning as she watched over both the flock and her three children. Dressed in bright peasant gear she held up a distaff like a big stick of candy floss and spun a heavy, flat stone suspended below it. I brought back one of each kind of whistle, intending to learn to play them. I failed, and gave them to a lady who teaches woodwind at a college of music. She was very pleased.

The great sheep industry – on which the nation lived during the mediaeval years – had produced also another breed of men very different from the quiet, withdrawn shepherds. If your name is Packer you should sigh for the deeds of some of your forebears.

Up on our own high sheep-walks there were no buildings other than the shepherds' huts except the great wool-barns, of which some still stand. In the pens around them the sheep were gathered at shearing-time. The fleeces, each tied in a twist of its own wool, were sown with a crescent-shaped pack needle into big hessian bags. These were the famous wool-sacks, so important once to the economy of Britain that the Lord Chancellor still sits on one in the House of Lords. It was to transport these riches that the packers arrived. They would gallop into view, shouting and whistling to their ferocious guard dogs and smacking their whips as they rode their sharp little galloways either side of a long line of heavier pack-cobs all tied nose-to-tail. Thousands of miles of the green droves throughout the interior of Britain were constantly travelled by the packers and the cattle drovers. When in the War the thin soil on the hill-tops was ploughed up for the first time there were turned up all along these ways early horseshoes, each like a split ace-of-spades cut out of iron plate.

The packers were a hard lot – because they had to be. The wealth of the nation travelled in their hands. Right back to times before history, when everything had to be moved that way, they had faced all the dangers of the wild places and known that their reputation depended on everything entrusted to them arriving safely. They knew also that the best way to avoid danger is to spread terror.

It would have been a sight to see them, the long line of packhorses each dwarfed by two great woolsacks – like a giant caterpillar driven by a swarm of wasps. It was not a sight that country-people liked to see coming down the hill into the village, about as welcome as a posse of trail-weary cowboys arriving in Dodge City.

There were inns along their routes that hung a wool-sack outside as a sign that they would be served, and perhaps as a warning to others to drink elsewhere for a while. The villagers were glad when the packers moved on. They could breathe a sigh of relief and unlock their daughters.

Yet, when money had to cross the country to pay taxes or large debts it was the custom to entrust it to the packers. The highwaymen didn't want to know about them. Gradually they developed the system of putting the money into safe-keeping at the start and paying what was due from what they received at the end of the journey. It is no

accident that one of the Big Five Banks is named after a
family that used to work the green roads from Wales to
London. Whatever they were they were born winners.

Once a year the gipsies moved in. There were always
two or three families around and we knew them very well
but strange gipsies arrived in large numbers for the potato-
picking. I don't suppose we could have got the potato crop
without them. There were no potato harvesting machines.
Either a single-horse ridge-plough would turn the rows
over; or the spinning lifter, working with the power of a
pair of horses would thrash two rows at a time out of the
ground and leave them lying on the surface. Either way
they had to be picked up by hand. The gipsy women would
take a row each and work down it bent double with legs
wide astride, picking the potatoes into the pockets of their
sack-apron, emptying them at intervals into the standing
sacks. The children worked too, three to a row, using flat
hazel potato baskets that had been made in preparation
for the season and hung in bundles on the carts when they
arrived. It was mainly the women and children who did
the work. The men seemed to turn out reluctantly, and
often not at all. This gave rise to a general anxiety as to
where they were and what they were doing.

However well we got on with our local families, there
is no doubt that in those days the gipsies had to be regarded
as a criminal community. Particularly the young boys. It
was evident that their social status depended on what they
could steal. I had a gipsy friend who, when he came to
call on me, left his children locked up in the front of his
box-van for the duration of the visit. They sat with their
noses pressed to the glass and their little black eyes
examined every inch and corner of our property. In the end
I said to him, 'Why don't you bring the kids in?'

He looked surprised. 'Sure you don't mind?' he said. He clearly could take no responsibility for what they did behind his back.

We saw the gipsies at close quarters because we were on the job next to them. Miss Harrison's school was always on holiday for potato-picking. They were exciting because they clearly belonged to somewhere else. They were dark-skinned and had sun-wrinkles round their eyes. They seemed to be weatherproof and very, very hard. It happened at one potato-picking that a woman got up from her row and walked to the hedge, to come back an hour later with a new-born baby. Perhaps less surprising, though, in our district than in an urban one. We were used to an old cow calving nonchalantly in twenty minutes and then going back to her grazing.

The grown-ups got worried if we became too interested in the gipsies. We were strictly forbidden to go near the encampments. It was still believed that gipsies kidnapped children. Once when she saw me beside the common staring at the gipsy camp Miss Harrison got off her bicycle to move me on my way.

It never happened; but over the years both a young fellow and a girl disappeared with the small travelling circus that made an annual visit to the district.

For me that circus was a place of humiliation. At an age when we used to make our pocket money breaking and schooling ponies, I decided to win the five pound prize they offered to anyone who could ride the unrideable mule. Five pounds – two weeks wages for a grown man! Confidently I strode into the ring and got on its back. The handlers let go and seven seconds later I was on my back seeing stars. It took a lot of living down.

Of the two who went away with the circus the girl was

pursued by her parents and brought home again. The fellow disappeared forever into the great world outside.

When people did go they usually went far away. On the small farms there were big families, many sons but only a single inheritance. The younger ones had to find their way into the skilled trades, or into the mines and mills of the valleys. Those who couldn't settle for those places still went to the Empire. I had an uncle who went to Fall River City, Massachusetts, taking with him all the savings that the family could spare; and a number of other things that we didn't miss till afterwards. I had another Uncle whom I saw only once and then in khaki. He had gone to Canada before I was born and when the war brought him back, he called on us for an hour on the way to the troopship. Within a week he was dead by the River Somme.

Countrymen had always gone to war, as the Old Man did to South Africa, but it was the two Great Wars that took them away in very large numbers; and this was a great contributor to all the changes.

I too went to war and worked my way round the world. I came back to find that the private worlds had gone and nowadays in the country everyone lives next to someone who has come from somewhere else.

That time which used to be an unconfining thing is now inaccurate if it varies by three seconds a day. And the chips of crystal have us all imprisoned in a machine in which there are no secrets, and from which there is no escape.

12
Only Yesterday

A lady in the village, the widow of an imperial functionary, said to me, 'I think I'm now the oldest inhabitant. I've been here twenty-four years.'

'Really', I said, 'but I've been talking to an old man who was born here.'

She showed some confusion. I should have understood that her meaning had not included the natives.

It seems only yesterday – though it is more than half a century – that I lived in a place where nearly all the inhabitants had been born. A few had been brought over by marriage from a pony's distance away. People had no need to get to know one another. That had been achieved long ago, in the playground at Miss Harrison's.

This was so not just in the countryside. The troop of soldiers that I joined in 1940 had all been born in one place. they had all joined the Territorials from two streets in the East End of London. The fellows had married the girls opposite and moved in with their parents. Granny lived next door. Their grandfathers were remembered in the two corner pubs that they frequented, and you could tell by listening to their talk whether they belonged to the Marquis of Granby or the other. Sometimes, when drink had flowed, there would be a set-to between the two communities, just as had been customary on their home pavements on a Saturday night.

It had been the same in our villages. If lads from a neighbouring one wandered over the border we would

throw stones at them. If one of them came alone and un-
supported and we had him outnumbered, we would dump
him in the brook. All in a spirit of fun, you understand.

After Dunkirk, when I sat behind the South Coast with
the London soldiers waiting for the Germans, the night
sky to the north was filled with a red glow. They knew
that their families were now in the thick of the battle and
they ran out in the morning to meet the milk-lorries and
ask where the bombs had dropped.

When they went back to the Smoke many of their villages
were just rubble-patches on which the Sweet Rosebay Willow-
herb had already established itself. They wrote me heart-
broken letters to say that it would never be the same again.
Worst of all, it seemed, they had lost their beloved trams.
I remembered driving through Kent in Battle of Britain
time and coming on a mob of East End hop-pickers filling
the square outside a country pub. They were drinking from
jugs and cans and babies' potties – the landlords wouldn't
trust them with glasses. They were singing their hearts
out and doing Knees Up, Mother Brown.

'Good God!' I said to Sergeant Reynolds, 'what a sight!
You wouldn't be surprised to see a tram come round the
corner!'

"'old on a bit governor,' he said. 'Don't break my bloody
'eart!'

For them, in their demob suits, the plans for the tower-
blocks and the new towns were already on the drawing
board.

For me, I found the big Shire Horses going to the butcher
to ease the meat rationing. The tractors had crossed the
Atlantic in the Liberty ships and farming was in hock to
fuel oil.

The city 'villages' had died in a few weeks of bombardment

and the new living places that were to replace them – part of the Socialist dream that was being promised in the days of demobilisation – were to be physically quite different. Nobody knew then how austere they would prove to be, or that life in them would have a barrenness that would contribute strongly to future dreams of the countryside. My London soldiers had no dream of the countryside. They frankly hated the place.

The changes to the country villages were slower and in some senses less obvious – on the picture-postcards, for instance. Many estates broke up and the land was bought by farmers with bank overdrafts, or by finance houses with pension funds. Those estates that continued took their land back in hand as the tenants died and handed it over to farm management companies. The subsidies that were born to feed the nation in war were juggled in and out of time with the politics of cost-of-living and the computers of Brussels. The chemical industry produced drugs for the land that would kill or change or stimulate almost every natural process. The tractors grew in horsepower every year and greatly elaborated their functioning until this year the whole area used for hay-making on one of our local farms which used to take five men three weeks was finished by one man in five days.

A quarter of a million skilled men have gone out of agriculture and the remaining heavy horses are put into special small zoos of their own where they can be visited by tourists.

Nowadays every second house in the village is being worked on. Thatchers are busier than ever. Builders buy the tiles from all the old barns and charge them up dear for mending village roofs. Blacksmiths work full time on decorative ironwork, and you can get a lot of money for an old oak beam that came out of the byre. All this is being paid for by people who were born elsewhere, and go elsewhere to earn more. The hardest thing is to get leave to build a small contemporary house, as each squire did in turn for his tenants.

The big yellow machines dig one trench after another up the street, constantly improving the services and leaving a pattern of parallel tarmac stripes. A man from the Council told me that whatever they do brings complaints either of neglecting the community or of 'endangering village life'. 'Village life!' he snorted. He was the son of a dairyman.

In a recent survey taken from the pub window, six out of ten women were seen to pass by in high-heeled shoes, and three of the rest were in trainers. Yet it seems only yesterday that the village street was dust and broken-stone and potholes full of water, and down one side of it ran an open brook with little flagstone bridges at the garden gates. In those days Granny's pattens were still in the porch for her to step into when she went outside.

Only yesterday we had a cricket on the hearth chirruping away the winter evenings. A lady who moved in said to me lately, 'We've got a thing in the house that makes a squeaky noise. Just by the fireplace. I think it's alive. What do I do, send for the Pest Officer?' I explained to her that the House Cricket is the luckiest of all spirits and that as long as you have him fiddling away from a crack in the inglenook you can look forward to a happy family life. Now I think she's going to put him in the inventory.

Just yesterday we dug a deep well because the Old Man wanted a better source of water than the spring where the white frog lived. He had bought the little barn-engine and planned a run of belting down the wall of the dairy to a pump that would fill a tank in the attic. Thus we should move up the social scale by having an upstairs bathroom.

Yes, we had the water-diviner and he found the right place, and the well-digger who, to my astonishment, started to lay the brick lining from the top, supporting each course in turn while he dug down a bit deeper. He wasn't going to risk the whole thing falling in on him.

Between them they had made wells for cottages all their working lives. Now you can't dig a well without a licence; and if you've got one your grandfather dug you may well be charged rates for it. Perhaps one day a man with reflectors on his roof may be fined for taking too much heat from the sun.

Only yesterday when the frost and the wind brought clumps of House Leek down off the old tiles, Grandmother gathered them up and dried them for her store of remedies. Her reputation was very high in this regard and people really believed in her. Perhaps her air of wisdom and secrecy contributed to her undoubted success. If your nose was stuffed up she gave you a snuff ground in a mortar from dried leaves of Basil. Poultices of Comfrey leaves gathered by the river were wrapped around sprained ankles and little packs of boiled Fennel were put on sore eyes. Rhubarb for constipation, Tormentil for sore gums and Nasturtium for troubles with the water. Elder, in the form of a strong, mulled wine, produced perspiration to drive out a fever.

When the Old Man came back from South Africa in a hospital ship she made him a pillow stuffed with Rosemary to keep away his nightmares. She herself constantly took Chervil for her memory, in case she should forget to gather all her materials at the appropriate times. Apart from all her herbal wisdom she was believed to have been not above a bit of mediaeval magic. They say that, secretly, she got rid of the wart on Horace White's nose by touching it with a frog. Certainly I can remember when it suddenly wasn't there any more.

Life yesterday was full of natural substances. Miss Hobbs at the shop sold locust beans and liquorice. Little triangular bags of sherbet that could be sucked out through one corner. Her toffee was in flat slabs the shape of the pans it had been made in and she cut it up for weighing with a pair of scissor-like snippers. These served also to attack the tall cones of white sugar that arrived in the thick paper dunces' caps into which it had been poured. Modern marketing came to Miss Hobbs's when she started to keep packets of sugar cubes.

The dry goods were all on benches along the wall, in little linen sacks with the tops rolled neatly down as I now see done only by an Arab spice-dealer in the souk. Every purchase was a matter of weights and measures – potatoes and apples by the half-bushel, peppercorns by the peck and cabbage seed by the half-ounce.

Miss Hobbs could deal with a shopful of customers while absorbing and exchanging the news and gossip. Yet she still found time – as they say in the women's magazines – to bake fresh every day her famous milk scones. These were an unforgettable delicacy and were eaten in a dozen houses before they were fully cooled from her oven. Such few as were left overnight became the perquisite of the ponies next day, and there were not many of them who would willingly drive on past. Certainly our donkey once dropped anchor ouside Miss Hobbs on a Sunday and took some moving on.

Yesterday we used to pick up the new tunes from the butcher-boys. From 'Goodbye, Dolly Gray' through to 'The Galloping Major', 'Never the Blushing Bride' and 'They wouldn't believe me', they plugged the latest hits along their routes. The tunes were made hits by music-hall artistes in endless tours of little town theatres, then given their final distribution along with chops and the sirloin. You don't hear many people who can whistle nowadays, let alone such virtuosos as the butcher-boys. When a lad developed a new trill he would try it out on every customer. In the days before frigidaires it was their job to get the meat from cold-room to kitchen as fast as possible and the clatter of their coming was unmistakable.

Nowadays they might say 'What a shame that boys should have to work at that age!' But they had a place in society. They were saucy little blighters but never delinquent. With their high, brightly painted carts and fiercely trotting ponies, the hours spent at high speed and the nerve to corner like Grand Prix drivers, and all heads turned to pick up their tunes, they had no need to seek further release of aggression.

But then, with crystal and cat's-whisker we began to listen to the Savoy Orpheans Band. Our tunes thence forward came not from the cockney music-hall but from New York's Tin Pan Alley. 'California here I come' and 'Seminola'. And a T Model Ford with the butcher's name on it.

The telegraph-boy lasted a bit longer, with his kepi cap and red bicycle; but unlike the butcher-boy he rarely brought happiness and satisfaction. Apart from the occasional birth of a baby or a betrothal, or an exam passed, the telegrams – like the TV News of nowadays – dealt in disaster. 'No bridegroom at the church turned up,' said one of the butcher-boy songs, 'but a telegraph-boy with his nose turned up!' His double knock was dreaded in the smaller houses. He knocked on our door in 1915 and told us the sad news of Uncle Holmes.

Yet none of this is really yesterday. Yesterday is much

further away than that. If it is twenty-five years between father and son, and fifty years between grandfather and grandson, then everything could be told, person-to-person, from the Black Death until today in sixteen conversations. There was a man alive in our village on the day I was born who remembered the death of Napoleon.

For all those people who speak of conserving the countryside, who love to walk and drive through it, yesterday is 1348. The countryside before that date is not to be recognised from today's Christmas cards. Here and there in the untouched wilderness were patches of open fields, each the width of a furlong – one furrow long, the length that an ox-team could pull a plough without resting for a breather. Around them there were just three kinds of buildings, baronial halls, hovels and churches – none of the cottages that people do up today with great respect for the original.

In the waste between they hunted the deer and cut timber while the swineherds drove the pigs, keeping a wary eye for the wild, white cattle and the bears that preyed on them.

Even the major rivers were scarcely to be distinguished. The fallen trees blocked them so that they spread into wide boggy areas into which the cranes flew every year and where the osprey fished. A beaver-dam blocked the River Kennet on the site of Newbury High Street with its traffic lights; and only here and there where the towns had pushed back the wilderness were the first stone bridges built. This was England only sixteen live conversations ago.

Even in the short time since it has taken many changes to produce the countryside as people now defend it. It took the two hundred years that wool was our staple export for the sheep to clear the thorns from the hills and create what is now called the natural turf of the downlands. In the Old Man's time W. H. Hudson, in *A Shepherd's Life*, still wrote of shepherds struggling to free the long-wooled sheep from the thorns. Now, with the advance of technology, the downs have gone under the plough.

Most of the hedges that farmers are attacked for grubbing out were planted in the eighteenth century, and at the time a Northamptonshire poet – because poetry was then the medium of protest – wrote angrily about the new-fangled hedges that were cutting up the beautiful, open countryside.

Successively, at quite long intervals, potatoes, tomatoes, Brussels sprouts and many other things have been added to the diet that comes from a country garden.

And how long is this moment at which time is called upon to stop? It is less than one two-hundredth of the time since we appeared after the Ice Age. If it were 24 hours since that happened, then our present countryside has been recognisable for just over six minutes.

Can changes cease? Does anyone drive down Newbury High Street and sorrow for the beavers? Is the corncrake, to which we listened every summer evening of our childhood, a better bird than the collared dove which has just come to live with us after a century's journey across Europe? Is it good that people should eat frozen vegetables? Is it bad that, because chickens are now kept in broiler-houses, they have become once again a food for everybody?

13

Crescendo

Back in the days when all television was black and white I was talking, in a series about the future, to an American Professor of Sociology. I said to him, 'How many people do you think there ought to be?'

The television critic of *The Observer*, a nice man with whom I had often been fishing, wrote that the question was outrageous. 'Not even God,' he said, 'should be permitted to ask that question.'

In the fourteenth century when our present countryside began to develop there were perhaps four million people in Britain. When I was born there were forty-five. Now there are over sixty million.

Seven out of ten people live in cities, and a friend of mine calculated that if everyone decided to go to the countryside for the weekend, and spread themselves out with perfect evenness over the surface of the realm, they would be eighty yards apart. There would be two of them on my little holding. Thirty of them visible in the farmer's fields opposite. And since the calculation refers to the whole surface of the land – mountains, motorways and mudflats included – there would no doubt be several hundreds treading water eighty yards apart in Lake Windermere.

It took fifty thousand years to produce the first billion human beings. The fourth billion was achieved in fourteen years and was announced just before my seventieth birthday. So I have a reasonable chance of seeing the fifth.

When I was young Aldous Huxley imagined, in *Brave*

New World, that one day the majority of children would have to be given conditioning courses in Rural Abhorrence in order to wash away any desire to move out of the glass-roofed, air-conditioned cities that would then be provided for them. Better perhaps to face the question 'If we are to have a countryside, how much will that countryside stand?'

Curiously the agrarian culture into which I was born and which is now dying, had within itself the seed of its own destruction. When the first patches of Emmer wheat were planted in the Middle East they marked the start of agriculture and, at the same time, signalled the inevitable end of country living.

The human race has been farming for about one-twentieth of its time on earth. Before that men lived as hunter-gathers and – in favourable circumstances – needed around two thousand acres to keep a family alive. And all the family had to work at it. Except for short periods, like the spring when all the birds nested or the autumn when all the fruits came, they had to work at it full-time. They moved like a herd of grazing deer around their territory to fresh ground every few days. No one survived who couldn't keep up. In later days they gathered semi-domesticated herds, but this only increased the distance and the frequency of their nomadic travels.

Then suddenly about five thousand years ago, in the neighbourhood of Jericho, there was a village. A group of people living in one place. They were farming. Now that crops could be grown instead of gathered from the wild, and animals could be husbanded instead of hunted or herded, a family could live on twenty-five acres. For the first time food for all the people could be provided by some of the people. There was a surplus.

No doubt at first this just meant that those who could not keep up with the hunting and gathering now had a chance to survive. They could work in a stationary way and develop the crafts. Even in my infancy most of the village cobblers and tailors and saddlers were cripples.

As agriculture improved its ability to support more than its own workers, the opportunities of the world opened up to those who were not engaged in it. The other characters in the drama of civilisation made their entrances. Soldiers, who replaced border quarrels with real war in pursuit of resources and made it possible for a few to rule the many. Priests, who demanded the building of temples from which they could disseminate a fear of divinity. Clerks, who set up their exchequer boards in counting houses. Artists, who dramatised the magical ideas of religion and astrologers who walked the path that led to the highway of science.

All of them were supported by the farming surplus. They had opportunism and intelligence. They were winners and they realised very early that the agriculturists must not be allowed to distribute their own surplus. The earliest buildings of the Sumerian rulers were great storehouses to which all grain had to be brought for distribution according to the King's will. They realised soon that the land was the key and founded the idea that the land must belong to the great while those who worked it must be kept humble. This idea was sustained successfully for five thousand years. In Britain, in Queen Victoria's reign, Richard Jefferies wrote *Hodge and his Masters* in which he showed reverence for the grandeur and bounty of the land and withering contempt for the farm-workers.

It next became clear, although all riches came from the surplus, the hauling of grain and produce was too clumsy a means of exchange for the wide distribution of goods and for international trade. So money was invented as a symbol of work and goods – only to become in no time a commodity in its own right. The earliest relic found in a village near to ours is a silver penny of King Aethelred, two minters having been ordered to the place in his reign together with a stock of fifty pounds of silver. Thus, I suppose, money was injected into the countryside at hundreds of places, to find its way back into all the trades and enterprises and extravagances that belonged to the civilisation made possible by farming.

In that civilisation the crescendo of human population rose. For two reasons they needed people. They needed great land armies. France with its land frontiers and the tradition of Napoleon's Grande Armée was the first country to introduce family allowances. And they needed huge numbers of factory workers. America, when its economy came off the prairies and began to industrialise, imported more than four million European workers in a decade.

Then, quite suddenly it seemed to me, as science and technology and finance spread like a systemic herbicide into all the veins of life, there came a time when many things could be done easier and better without the aid of people. Starting first in the developed countries millions of people began to find their lives purposeless. In the double-talk of civilisation they were comforted with the idea of 'increased leisure'; and in line with the 'developed' approach there was talk of a 'Leisure Industry', a phrase that would have seemed inexplicable a short while earlier.

But purposelessness brings unease and anxiety – not to be more than temporarily assuaged by sun-bathing on the Costa Brava. Obsession with human rights arises from a suspicion that progress is making people less important.

The Caring Society, a fantasy contrasting strangely with the way people now treat one another, can be just a sublimation of the fear of being oneself unwanted.

The sadness of not being able to have purposeful work in one's own hands has been seen not only among thousands of industrial workers but also among the older men of the countryside.

Farming itself has been so developed that, while the number of farmers has fallen by a third, the surplus has become so great as to be an embarrassment in the Western world where the constrictions of finance make it difficult to distribute it to those who still need it. The farming industry on which the whole of civilisation rested is enmeshed – like Laocoon and his serpents – in politics, finance and the problems of fossil fuel supply. As to the farm-workers, seventy-five per cent of them were – to use the American euphemism – 'let go' within a lifetime. Their only memorial is a determination to preserve their habitat shown by people who want to look at it and walk its footpaths in such numbers that, in certain places, they are having to be sprayed with a plastic binder – even though the path in question may first have come into being because, at one season of the year, two or three families of woodmen needed to make their way up to their lettings in the copse.

In later years I saw Aldous Huxley in person. At the University of California I heard him give one of the last lectures of his life. He was crouched over a table under a reading lamp, squinting through a hand-lens at his manuscript that was entitled 'The problems of human numbers'. I have that lecture recorded and I play it at intervals. For one thing, the style is simple and perfect. In the whole lecture on the subject he never used the word 'population'. There was no housing problem, he said, only a problem of human numbers. No problems of transport or education – all such were just symptoms – only a problem with human numbers. Man, who had faced all problems of conquering nature fearlessly was simply unable to face the problem of himself.

Then perhaps we should address ourselves to the question that I was admonished for asking. As a matter of fact I did again ask it of a University Vice-Chancellor with whom I was having lunch. To my surprise he told me, speaking rather guardedly, that he knew the answer.

He had served, he said, for a long time on a committee that had been asked by some organ of government to consider what the optimum population of Britain might be in the days of our grandchildren. Taking all that was known and all that research was seeming to indicate, and all that hundreds of expert witnesses were inclined to postulate, they were to conclude how many people would be able to live full and happy lives in the Britain of that time. All to be healthy and well-educated. All to have purposeful things to do and leisure in a proper amount. All to possess the goods that would then be available, enough space to preserve them from the stress of density, houses that would give them comfort, services that would see all the tasks of civilisation done.

'And did you find an answer?'

'Yes, as good an answer as could be found, bearing in mind all the things that were not yet known.'

'And when it your committee going to report?'

'It has reported.'

'And when is the report to be published?'

'Never, of course. We thought the answer was thirty-six million. There are sixty-five million alive now. What democratic politician could even approach the problem of getting rid of twenty-nine million people?'

So perhaps I – or even God – can never think of asking the outrageous question. Perhaps man is just a blind horse with the bit between his teeth who can't be stopped until he hits a hay-barn.

It's a funny thing that, only yesterday, the thrill we felt as we climbed into the market-cart every Wednesday arose from the fact that, just once in a week, we were going to meet some people other than ourselves.

Also by Jack Hargreaves and published by the Dovecote Press

OUT OF TOWN

A Life Relived on Television

Out of Town was published in 1987 to immediate critical acclaim, and quickly became a bestseller throughout the country. The long-awaited autobiography of Jack Hargreave's childhood and early youth, it superbly evokes the rural pastimes and pleasures that shaped his television programmes. Moving, humorous, always readable, it delightfully evokes a world and way of life that has now vanished. 8 pages of illustrations.

'His small-screen interpretations of country life as lived in his boyhood are vividly redistilled . . . '

ISBN 0 946159 46 7   *180 pages*
216 x 138mm   *Paperback £5.95*

Copies of this or any other book published by The Dovecote Press can be ordered from booksellers throughout the United Kingdom, or in cases of difficulty direct from The Dovecote Press, Stanbridge, Wimborne, Dorset, BH21 4JD